THE
BHAGAVAD GITA

*Translated from the Sanskrit
with introduction and notes by*

B. Srinivasa Murthy

Revised Second Edition

Foreword by

Christopher Chapple

LONG BEACH PUBLICATIONS

POST OFFICE BOX 14807
LONG BEACH, CALIFORNIA 90803

Books by the same author:

East-West Encounters in Philosophy and Religion edited by
Ninian Smart and B. Srinivasa Murthy.

Mahatma Gandhi and Leo Tolstoy Letters, edited with introduction
and notes by B. Srinivasa Murthy.

Martin Heidegger in Conversation, edited by Richard Wisser,
translated by B. Srinivasa Murthy.

Mother Teresa and India

Library of Congress Cataloging-in-Publication Data

Bhagavadgītā. English.
   The Bhagavad Gita / translated from the sanskrit with
introduction and notes by B. Srinivasa Murthy ; foreword by
Christopher Chapple. — Rev. 2nd ed.
      p. cm.
   Includes bibliographical references.
   ISBN 0-941910-05-9 : $11.95
   I. Murthy. B. Srinivasa. II. Title.
BL1138.62.E5   1991a
294.5'924—dc20   90-82501
                                                      CIP

Copyright © 1985, 1991, 1995, 1998 by B. Srinivasa Murthy

Printed in the United States of America.

CONTENTS

With deep appreciation
and gratitude to:
my parents
Mary Jo Murthy
Professor F. J. von Rintelen
Dr. James Harper
Dr. Douglas McConnell

FOREWORD

The Bhagavad Gita coalesces drama and philosophy, poetry and religion. As the pivotal moment in a colossal tragedy, it evokes the collective spiritual memory of Indian civilization as embodied by the reflection and insight of Sri Krishna. The time of the *Gita* is sacred time. The event takes place in a state of suspended animation. The dialogue between Krishna and Arjuna requires the stoppage of all activity, a stoppage that is symbolic of and metaphorical for the cessation of conventional concerns to allow the emergence of highest consciousness. The text places a wedge in reality that interrupts the life flow of the reader. To pause to read of attachment and crisis yielding to detachment and bliss engenders in the reader the same: Gandhi knew this well, and retreated to this great song daily.

Dozens of translations of the *Gita* have been published over the years. Though this is a timeless text in its original Sanskrit, the reading of it into Western languages is framed and construed according to the translator's time and place and audience. Edgerton crafted a linguistic marvel, holding to the original word order and paving the way for generations of fledgling Sanskritists to be guided through the text into grammatical fluency. Radhakrishnan brought forth a translation that neatly fits certain philosophical expectations and anticipations of those steeped in European intellectual traditions. Christopher Isherwood rendered a fluid, magical combination of poetry and prose, leading his guru Swami Prabhavananda to proclaim that divine inspiration must surely have contributed. Antonio deNicholas used the *Gita* as a bridge between worlds, providing a basis for the exploration of self and culture regardless of one's native garb. Literateurs Ann Stafford and Winthrop Sargeant, to name just two, have revelled in the richness of language and abundance of universal philosophical imagery.

The translation of Srinivasa Murthy, like its predecessors, celebrates and pays homage to this great literary and philosophical work. Its use of language is clear and direct, and yet it challenges the reader to enter into the worldview of India. It becomes clear, for instance, that the spirit spoken of in the term *purusha* is defined not as a personal or substantialist soul but refers to a modality of heightened, spiritualized consciousness, referred to in the *Samkhya Karika* as the detached witness. *Prakriti* is not nature in an objective, scientific sense, but provides an accounting for all things that change, including such diverse entitites as personality, mood, food, physical realities, and various activities. Likewise, its three components—*sattva, rajas,* and *tamas*—defy facile translation. Srinivasa Murthy leaves these terms in their original, enticing the reader to expand his or her cosmology for the sake of authentically entering into the world of Krishna and Arjuna.

Unlike some earlier attempts, this translation is particularly well suited to the uninitiated. It provides a marvelous, concise introduction to the *Mahabarata*, the great epic of which the *Gita* is but one small part. It introduces the text with a summary survey of Hindu notions of self and karma, a synopsis of the Samkhya and Yoga schools of thought, and an overview of the paths of action, knowledge, and devotion. Conceived not from the perspective of an outsider looking in nor from the perspective of an insider seeking to mystify the curious, this book admirably makes accessible a great classic of world literature, in a manner true to the Indian tradition.

Christopher Chapple   December 1990
Loyola Marymount University   Los Angeles

PREFACE

While I was a student of philosophy at the University of Mysore in India, I heard a guest lecturer speak on "Sense, Reason and the Self in the *Gita*," which had a powerful impact upon me. Although I was familiar with this great work, the lecture gave me new insights and inspiration. Ever since that time, I have had an irresistible urge to translate the *Bhagavad Gita* anew, incorporating the flavor of the original Sanskrit into modern English. Hence, this translation came about.

I am greatly indebted to Sri. Swami Ganeshananda Saraswati of Hrishikesh, who delivered splendid lectures on "The Essence of the *Gita*" in the city of Hassan, India, in June 1985. I am especially thankful for Swami Ganeshananda Saraswati's generosity in taking time to discuss with me individually the key concepts in the *Gita*, as well as the interpretation of significant Sanskrit verses in the *Gita* and the Upanishads.

I owe a deep debt of gratitude to my professor, S. S. Raghavachar, of the University of Mysore, who gave me a strong foundation in Indian philosophy, as well as my doctoral advisor, Professor Fritz-Joachim von Rintelen, of the University of Mainz, West Germany, with whom I had many lively discussions on Indian and German philosophies from the comparative standpoint.

I would also like to thank Professor Jasper Blystone, Loyola Marymount University, Los Angeles, and Professor Gary Baran, Los Angeles City College, for their valuable comments and constructive criticisms on the manuscript. I am also highly obliged for the help given by Professors Daniel Guerriere, Peter Lowentrout, and Paul Tang, of California State University, Long Beach. I would also like to thank Mrs. Roberta Mathias for her efficient typing of the manuscript and Theresa Delaney for the fine cover design. Last but not least, special thanks to my wife, Mary Jo, for her enthusiastic involvement throughout the project.

September 1985   B. Srinivasa Murthy

PREFACE TO
THE SECOND EDITION

The second edition incorporates constructive comments made by my students and colleagues. The Introduction has been substantially revised, minor errors have been corrected in the translation, a Glossary has been added and the Bibliography has been expanded.

I am deeply indebted to Professor Christopher Chapple of Loyola Marymount University, Los Angeles, for his invaluable advice and meticulous review of the revisions. I would like to express special appreciation to my friends and colleagues for their critiques, especially to professors Gary Baran, Los Angeles City College; Ann Berliner, California State University, Fresno; Jasper Blystone, Loyola Marymount University, Los Angeles; Jeffrey Broughton, California State University, Long Beach; Hope Fitz, Eastern Connecticut State University; Christian Jochim, San Jose State University; and D.R. SarDesai, University of California, Los Angeles.

B. Srinivasa Murthy   January 1991
California State University, Long Beach

INTRODUCTION

The *Bhagavad Gita*, popularly known as the *Gita*, is one of the most important philosophical and religious classics in the world. The *Gita* synthesizes both rational analysis and religious inspiration in answering the fundamental questions of the meaning of life and death. It has inspired the Indian people for centuries, guiding them in their daily struggles and giving them spiritual strength to lead a life of goodness, tolerance and harmony. When faced with existential crises and critical life decisions, one can turn to the words of the *Bhagavad Gita* for direction and consolation. Mahatma Gandhi aptly summarized his indebtedness to this great work: "When disappointment stares me in the face and all alone I see not one ray of light, I go back to the *Bhagavadgita*. I find a verse here and a verse there and I immediately begin to smile in the midst of overwhelming tragedies—and my life has been full of external tragedies—and if they have left no visible, no indelible scar on me, I owe it all to the teachings of the *Bhagavadgita*."[1]

The impact of the *Gita's* teachings have been widespread, reaching far beyond the borders of India. As the nuclear physicist, Robert Oppenheimer,[2] watched the first stunning explosion of the atom bomb in tests conducted in New Mexico, he remembered the following words of the *Gita*: "If the light of a thousand suns were to blaze all at once in the sky, it would be like the splendor of that great Being" (11.12). The famous German philosopher-humanist, Wilhelm von Humboldt, commented that this classic is "the most beautiful, perhaps the only true philosophical song existing in any known tongue."³ Ralph Waldo Emerson, Henry David Thoreau, T.S. Eliot, Arthur Schopenhauer, Aldous Huxley, and Sir Edwin Arnold were all deeply influenced by the *Gita*.

The reason why the *Bhagavad Gita* has been so popular in India is due to the fact that it is both an inspirational and practical guide to daily living. The *Gita's* teachings are simple and direct, whereas most of the ancient Indian writings on philosophy and religion, in contrast, are accessible only to scholars. From the deep well of the *Gita*, both scholars and laymen can draw the waters of faith, reason, and natural law, in accordance with their individual needs.

The eighteen chapters of the *Gita* are taken from the third episode of the *Bhishmaparvan* (Book of Bhishma) in the *Mahabharata*. The authorship of the *Gita* is unknown, for it was customary for the ancient seers to place no claim on their writings. However, the authorship is attributed to Vyasa and the text has been estimated to have been written in the fifth century B.C.

THE BACKGROUND STORY

The background story leading up to the dialogue between Krishna and Arjuna is essential for the reader to become familiar with the key personalities involved, as well as the historical events heading towards the battle.

In a bygone age, there lived two cousins, who belonged to the royal family of the Bharata clan, namely Dhritarashtra and Pandu. Dhritarashtra was the elder cousin, but he was deprived of kingship because he was born blind and Pandu became the ruler of the Bharatas. Dhritarashtra married

Gandhari, a princess of Gandhara. Gandhara is today known as Kandhahar in Afghanistan. Dhritarashtra fathered one hundred sons, known as the Kauravas, of which Duryodhana was the first-born.

King Pandu had two wives. His first wife, Kunti, bore three sons, named Yudhisthira, Bhima and Arjuna, and his second wife, Madri, bore twins, named Nakula and Sahadeva. King Pandu died at an early age and Dhritarashtra became regent. The five sons of Pandu, known as the Pandava brothers, were brought up by Dhritarashtra.

Bhishma and Drona, the archer, guided the education of the Pandavas. All five brothers developed fine moral character, warrior skills and leadership qualities. Yudhisthira, the eldest of the five, was chosen to be the future ruler over the portion of the kingdom inherited from his father. Among the hundred sons of Dhritarashtra, the eldest, Duryodhana, was the favorite. Duryodhana was vicious, jealous, and cunning, whereas Yudhisthira, in contrast, was noble, gentle, kind and righteous.

As Prince Yudhisthira began to learn kingly duties, Prince Duryodhana became increasingly jealous and enraged. He began plotting to destroy the Pandava brothers and usurp their share of the kingdom. One of Duryodhana's plots was to construct a house built of wax and other flammable materials and then trick the five brothers into residing there. He intended to burn down the house and be rid of them once and for all. Fortunately, the intended victims learned of the plot and fled, disguised as Brahmin mendicants. To escape the evil-minded Duryodhana, the Pandavas went into hiding and wandered from place to place.

One day, the five brothers were surprised to come across an unusual contest, which was open to all men. The competition was an intricate archery contest and the winner would be rewarded with the honor of marrying King Drupada's beautiful daughter, Draupadi. A fish was suspended on a pole high in the air above a large basin of water. Each contestant had to look at the fish's reflection in the basin of water and attempt to shoot his arrow through the eye of the fish. Only five shots were allowed. Of course, Duryodhana did his best to win the princess, but he failed, as did numerous other competitors. Then, Arjuna stepped up to the basin and pierced the eye of the fish with his first shot. Arjuna married Princess Draupadi and, with King Drupada's support, the Pandavas returned to their kingdom. However, King Dhritarashtra gave back only half of the Pandava's legal inheritance and kept the remainder for his own sons. Yudhisthira became king of Indra Prastha, which is near New Delhi.

Prince Duryodhana, in collusion with his uncle, Sakuni, hatched another plan to dethrone King Yudhisthira and obtain his inheritance. Sakuni was an expert dice player and Yudhisthira's one weakness was his terrible passion for gambling. Duryodhana arranged for his father, King Dhritarashtra, to invite Yudhisthira for a game of dice. But when the game began, Dhritarashtra had Sakuni play in his place with loaded dice. In the heat of the game, Yudhisthira bet his entire kingdom and lost! However, through the intervention of Krishna, Dhritarashtra agreed to return the kingdom to Yudhisthira.

At a later date, King Dhritarashtra again invited King Yudhisthira to a dice game. Duryodhana and Sakuni devised elaborate stakes for this game. The losing side must live in the forest for twelve years and go into hiding in the thirteenth year. If they are discovered during the thirteenth year, they must submit to another twelve years of exile in the forest. If the losers successfully conceal their identities throughout the thirteenth year, they may return and reclaim their kingdom and position.

Yudhisthira, caught up in gambling fever, agreed to the bet and lost again. This time, the Pandavas had to fulfill the agreement and they went to live in the forest, leaving their lands and riches behind.

After enduring the years of exile and hiding their identities throughout the thirteenth year, the brothers returned to reclaim their kingdom. By that time, Duryodhana had become the ruler and he refused to give up the Pandavas' kingdom. The Pandava brothers were enraged by this injustice and both sides prepared for war.

The *Bhagavad Gita* begins as the two sides face each other in full battle array. Sanjaya, the king's minister, relates to the blind Dhritarashtra all that is taking place on the battle ground. As the two armies are lined up and ready for the first clash of arms on the battlefield of Kurukshetra, Arjuna and his charioteer, Lord Krishna, begin the dialogue which makes up the *Gita*.

Lord Krishna is the most important figure in the *Bhagavad Gita*, for he is God in human form. Although Krishna appears to be Arjuna's charioteer, he is the incarnation of Lord Vishnu, one of the gods in the Hindu trinity. Many mythological legends have been recorded in the *Bhagavata* about Lord Krishna's entry into the world of men and his early life. In the *Gita*, Arjuna represents the typical human being and Krishna, as the Supreme Lord of the universe, teaches Arjuna how to seek perfection and realize the Divine.

The major teachings woven together in the *Bhagavad Gita* have their roots in ancient Indian texts, primarily the Vedas, the Upanishads, and the Sankhya and Yoga systems. An overview of these teachings is presented in the following pages.

THE INFLUENCE OF THE UPANISHADS

The influence of the Upanishads upon the *Bhagavad Gita* is very significant. In fact, the *Gita* can be classified as a separate Upanishad. A.B. Keith considers the *Gita* to have originally been an Upanishad similar to the *Shvetashvatara Upanishad*. Even though the *Gita* forms part of the epic *Mahabharata*, its central teachings are more philosophical and religious than the rest of the *Mahabharata*.

The main teachings of the Upanishads, namely, the nature of *Brahman* or *Atman* (the Universal Self or Soul) and *atman* (the individual self or soul), form the basis of the most salient doctrine in the *Gita*. The immortality of the Self, the distinction between the individual self and the absolute Self, the bondage of the self and reincarnation, and the way in which the transcendence of the self can be achieved, all form the life blood of the *Gita*.

Frequently, the passages found in the *Gita* have been directly absorbed from the Upanishads. For example, in the *Katha Upanishad* we read: "The Self is not born, It does not die. It has not come from anywhere, nothing has come from It. Unborn, eternal, everlasting, primal, It is not slain when the body is slain" (*Katha Up.* 1.2.18). The *Gita* presents the same idea: "It is never born, nor does It die at anytime; nor, having once been, will It again cease to be. It is unborn, eternal, permanent and primal. It is not slain when the body is slain" (2.20). Again, the *Katha Upanishad* states: "If the slayer thinks he slays and if the slain one thinks he is slain, neither of them understand. The Self slays not, nor can It be slain" (*Katha Up.* 1.2.19). The *Gita* reiterates: "He who understands that this Self is a slayer, and he who understands that It is slain; neither of them have wisdom. The Self neither slays nor is slain'' (2.19).

We find innumerable parallels between the *Mundaka*, the *Isa*, and the *Shvetashvatara Upanishads* and the *Bhagavad Gita* on the subjects of ritualism, sacrifice, action and the practice of yoga, as well as the way to Brahman.

The Upanishadic texts form the last part of the Vedas. Vedic concepts have also directly influenced the *Bhagavad Gita's* ideas, particularly on the subjects of revealed knowledge, *Purusha* (spirit), *dharma*, and the four castes. The *Gita* contains two remarkable chapters on *Raja Yoga* (mysticism) and *Vibhuti Yoga* (the manifestation of the Divine). The description of Lord Krishna's divine manifestations, found in Chapter 10 of the *Gita*, strongly resembles both the style and content of the description of the Supreme Being found in the *Rig Veda*.

THE SELF

One of the most important teachings of the *Gita* is on the nature of the Universal Self and the individual self. *Atman* (the Universal Self) residing in a human being is known as *atman* (the individual self). Both the *Gita* and the *Upanishads* present discourses on the nature of the Self from various perspectives.

In the *Chandogya Upanishad*, a story is told about six well-read scholars who assembled together to discuss the question, ''Who is our *Atman*?'' '' After a spirited discussion, they decided to consult with a scholar named Aruni, who had studied the Universal *Atman*. When the six presented Aruni with their problem, he was taken aback because he feared that he would not be able to answer the difficult questions which they would pose. So Aruni suggested that they all go to Kaikeya, a well-versed scholar on *Atman*.

Kaikeya asked each scholar individually to express his concept of the Universal *Atman*. One explained that he venerated the sky as the Universal *Atman*, another venerated the sun, and yet another, the wind. The remaining three scholars interpreted *Atman* as the waters, or the earth, or space itself. Kaikeya then pointed out that each had only partially grasped the concept of the Universal *Atman*. All six scholars had made the same serious error, for each perceived *Atman* to be only outside of himself when, in fact, It can also be found within him.

In the *Gita*, Arjuna is the symbolic representative of the individual self and Lord Krishna is the manifestation of the Universal Self. Arjuna's dilemma clearly illustrates the plight of the individual self which is beset by confusion and suffering in this world. Struggling with despondency and moral conflict, Arjuna asks Krishna why he should fight and kill his kinsmen, revered teachers, and friends. He begs Krishna to guide him in taking the correct action. While teaching Arjuna, Lord Krishna reveals various aspects of the value and meaning of human existence, of which the nature of the Self is paramount.

Krishna presents three main aspects of the Self: the immortality of the Self, the need for self-realization, and the method of self-realization. Since the Self is immortal, the questions of life and death should be viewed from that ultimate perspective. One can destroy the body but not the Self. Krishna advises Arjuna: "You have been grieving for those who should not be grieved for, yet you speak words about wisdom. The wise grieve neither for the living nor for the dead" (2.11) and, again, "he who understands that this self is a slayer, and he who understands that it is slain; neither of them have wisdom. The self neither slays nor is slain" (2.19). Lord Krishna elucidates further that nothing can harm the Self, for "weapons cannot cut It; fire cannot burn It; waters do not drench It; nor does the wind wither It" (2.23).

Socrates expressed the similar idea of the indestructible nature of the self in Plato's *Phaedo*. After Socrates was condemned to die, his follower, Crito, asked: " 'In what way shall we bury you, Socrates?' Socrates replied: 'In any way you like, but first you must catch me, the real me. . . . Be of good cheer, my dear Crito, and say that you are burying my body only, and do with that whatever is usual and what you think best.'"⁴

Man has the innate need to realize a higher destiny and to find meaning in existence. The longing to reach a plateau of peace and tranquility in the experience of daily living has been evident throughout history. Empirical knowledge, the satisfaction of sensual desires, and material possessions and achievements do not culminate in self-realization. Inner harmony and peace become a reality only when one realizes that the self is part of a greater Self. "Let a man raise himself by the Self, let him not degrade himself . . . for the Self alone is the friend of the self and the Self alone is the enemy of the self" (6.5). A routine existence, bogged down in every-dayness, rusts the mind and robs the spark of life. When we transcend the empirical conditions of our experience and reach a higher state of consciousness, we are able to accept any events in life with equanimity, whether success or failure, pleasure or pain, joy or sorrow.

The *Gita* presents a means for attaining self-realization through meditation. "Let the yogi at all times strive to concentrate his mind on the Supreme Self, remaining alone in solitude, self controlled and free from desires and posses-

sions'' (6.10). Krishna instructs Arjuna on the method to
follow: "Sitting there, concentrating his mind on a single
object, controlling his thought and the activity of the senses,
let him practice yoga for self purification" (6.12). Through
meditation and purification of the mind, the individual
gradually rises above the ordinary traumas of existence and
reaches inner tranquility.

The experience of the Self is not reserved for a select few
yogis but is possible for every seeker. In the *Gita*, the term
yogi has the specific meaning of "consistent endeavor aimed
at a specific goal." For "where thought enters into silence,
stilled by the practice of concentration, one sees the Self
through the self and is content in the Self" (6.20).

KARMA

The doctrine of *karma* has had a profound influence on
Indian philosophical and religious thought. *Karma* has various meanings, such as: action, activity, process, rite, and
past actions. In the *Gita*, the word *karma* has two meanings,
firstly as actions in this life and, secondly, the result of past
actions which determine a person's reincarnation and fate in
this life. The *Gita* deals only with the concept of reincarnation and does not address the subject of transmigration.

The doctrine of *karma*, as found in the Vedas and the
Upanishads, is infused throughout the *Gita*. The law of
karma states that we will become what we do and reap what
we sow. The person who performs good actions becomes
virtuous and, likewise, the one who does bad actions
becomes evil.

Karma is the cosmic force of moral cause and effect. It

should not be construed merely as the automatic recycler of souls. The doctrine of *karma* is fundamentally the application of the scientific law of causation to the spiritual plane. Every act performed by an individual has its inexorable consequences. *Karma* is established in one's past lives, operates in the present life and will continue to operate in the future. If proper steps are not taken to attain liberation from *samsara* (reincarnation), the wheel of *karma* continues to revolve.

Since *karma* is linked to past actions, it can be considered deterministic. Nonetheless, one has the moral freedom in the present life to offset bad *karma* through self-realization. Christopher Chapple, in his excellent book *Karma and Creativity*, remarks: "Through activity, the binding influences of the past are overcome and a new order, a new vision is brought forth, a new way of life anchored in creativity rather than mired in past actions."[5] Radhakrishnan writes that ". . . the cards in the game of life are given to us. We do not select them. They are traced to our past *karma* but we can call as we please, lead what suit we will and as we play, we gain or lose. And there is freedom . . ."[6] Although the theory of *karma* determines one's *kshetra* (field of action), it never determines one's mode of action. *Karma* is, therefore, more positive than normative and more descriptive than deterministic. According to the law of *karma*, no one escapes moral retribution, although the results of unethical action may not become immediately apparent. The only way to escape the meshes of past evil action is through selfless action. The past may be distressing but the future is filled with hope. Man is indeed the architect of his destiny and he has the power to mold his future. The author of the *Yoga Vasistha* says: "There is hardly anything in existence which is not attainable through right and earnest effort. . . . Through effort alone, the wise always come out of dangerous situations and not through the absurd belief in destiny.''

In the *Gita*, Lord Krishna advises Arjuna to carry on action in the spirit of *nishkama karma* (actionless action) and not to worry about the consequences. Krishna counsels Arjuna not to grieve for the inevitable because ''as the embodied self passes through childhood, youth and old age in the body, so does it pass into another body'' (2.13), and ''just as a person discards worn out clothes and puts on new ones, so too the embodied self casts off old and worn out bodies and enters into other new ones'' (2.22). Both birth and death are inevitable in the wheel of karma. The only escape from this cycle is to free oneself from attachment through meditation and through the unselfish performance of duty and sacrificial works.

The belief in *karma* and reincarnation has been a strong moral force in Indian society. Centuries ago, Shankara persuasively remarked that ''unless a person is aware of the existence of the self in a future life, he will not be inclined to attain what is good in this life and avoid what is evil.''[7]

THE SANKHYA SYSTEM

The doctrines of the early Sankhya had a major influence upon the *Gita*. The Gita has absorbed the main doctrine of *Purusha* and *Prakriti* in its entirety. ''Know that *Prakriti* (nature) and *Purusha* (spirit) are both beginningless and know also that the modes and forms are born of nature'' (13.19). The *Gita* recognizes the major principles of the Sankhya's evolutionary scheme, as well as a theistic superstructure. The Sankhya school eventually developed into a naturalistic and evolutionary system which does not recognize God, but the earlier Sankhya teachings were theistic. We find a splendid description of the higher and lower nature in the *Gita*. Lord Krishna says, "My material nature is eightfold: earth, water, fire, air, ether, mind, reason, and ego" (7.4). He further comments, "This is My lower nature, but also learn of My higher nature . . . which is the indwelling spirit by which this world is sustained" (7.5).

The *Gita* completely absorbs the concept of the three *gunas* (modes or qualities) which make up *Prakriti*, namely *sattva, rajas,* and *tamas,* and develops a scheme of human nature based upon these concepts. In the Sankhya system, *guna* means a 'component or constituent element,' whereas in the *Gita, guna* means 'mode or quality.'

HUMAN NATURE IN THE GITA

The concept of human nature found in the *Gita*, which has been borrowed from the Sankhya philosophy, is further expanded to present a general classification of personality types and a foundation for the evaluation of human behavior.

An underlying assumption of the *Gita's* analysis of human nature is that personalities carry certain traits which are inborn. An individual's potential character and attitude is manifested in actuality as trends of behavior and value orientation. The three types of persons are: the *sattvic*, in whom the quality of goodness predominates; the *rajasic*, in whom the quality of passion predominates; and the *tamasic*, in whom dullness and ignorance are the overriding characteristics. These three qualities are found in every

individual and the combination and permutation of the *gunas
(sattva, rajas,* and *tamas)* cause a person to behave according to his inner urges.

This description of human nature is deterministic and
somewhat fatalistic. Everyone is driven by the predominance
of *sattva, rajas,* or *tamas* and we are unable to go against
our own nature. As the *Gita* puts it: "Bound by your own
karma which is born of your own nature . . . that which
through delusion you wish not to do, even that you shall do
against your will" (18.60). However, the teachings of the
Gita also offer a positive means of escape from the deterministic wheel of *karma* and rebirth. Through the practice of
yoga, we can attain the discrimination to understand the
gunas. This knowledge then aids in overcoming the deficien-
cies within our own nature and developing the good in us.

A person of *sattvic* nature is depicted as the superior type
of personality. "*Sattva*, being pure, is luminous and
healthy. It binds (the soul) . . . by attachment to joy and
attachment to knowledge" (14.6). When *sattva* is dominant
in the person, the light of knowledge shines. Even the foods
which the *sattvic* person eats are those which increase life,
vitality and strength. The actions carried out by the *sattvic*
type are actions performed without attachment and without
seeking reward. A person of this type worships God
devoutly, closely follows the scriptures, and perceives the
one eternal Being in all beings. He is characterized by
evenness of mind and is undisturbed in both success and
failure. Only the person who has developed *sattva* as his
predominant trait has the potentiality for overcoming *karma*
and attaining liberation.

The *rajasic* person "is characterized by passion arising
from craving and attachment. It binds the embodied soul by
attachment to action" (14.7). When *rajas* is dominant, the

elements of greed, enterprise, restlessness, and passion exhibit themselves as main traits.

The *rajasic* type is utilitarian, success oriented, and ready to challenge and fight. At times, he can be obsessed with achieving his goal. "That firmness by which one clings with attachment to duty, pleasure and wealth, desiring rewards of action, that is of the nature of *rajas*" (18.34). The *rajasic* person is sensuous and passionate, regardless of the consequences. Even the foods he craves are pungent, bitter, sour, salty, and hot. The religious activities carried on by this type of person are done with the desire to obtain reward, for "that penance, which is performed in hypocrisy to gain honor, respect and reverence, is said to be *rajasic*. It is short lived and impermanent" (17.18).

The *tamasic* person, whom the *Gita* classifies as the lowest form of human nature, is characterized by inactivity and dullness. "Know that *tamas* is born of ignorance and it deludes all embodied beings, O Bharata. It binds through negligence, laziness and sleep" (14.8). There is no salvation for the one in whom *tamas* predominates because prudential judgment and rational deliberation are absent. "That action which is undertaken through ignorance, regardless of the consequences, loss or injury it may cause to others, and regardless of one's own ability, is said to be *tamasic*" (18.25). Again, even food habits reflect *tamas*, for the foods preferred are stale and tasteless. In other words, there is no sense of refinement or balance in the selection of food.

The penances and ceremonies performed by persons of *tamasic* nature have the traits of self torture and the worship of ghosts and devils. Frequently, their ceremonies are carried out with the evil intention of ruining other persons.

The *Gita*'s analysis of personality types gives us clues about trends of behavior. Proper knowledge and understand-

ing of the three *gunas* allow us to better understand human
nature.

THE SYSTEM OF YOGA

The early teachings of yoga, which have been incorporated
into the *Gita*, not only increase one's understanding of human
nature but, more importantly, provide an indispensable
method for reaching salvation. The teachings of the *Gita*
emphasize various paths, or yogas, which point the way toward salvation. Perfection may be attained through the yoga
of action, the yoga of knowledge, and the yoga of devotion.

In the later system of yoga, developed by Patanjali, *chitta*
(thought, intelligence, the mind) is subject to five types of
suffering, namely, *avidya* (ignorance), *asmita* (egotism),
raga (attachment), *dvesa* (aversion), and *abhinivesha* (the
fear of death). The bondage of the self comes about through
improper identification between *Purusha* and *Prakriti*, for
Purusha is changeless whereas *Prakriti* is forever changing.
The individual who is ignorant of the nature of *Prakriti* is
enslaved by suffering. The system of yoga corrects this
deficiency and explains how to overcome the five kinds of
suffering through control of breathing, control of the senses,
and meditation. The *Gita* integrates yoga into the path of
action through the relinquishment of the fruits of action.

The essential teachings presented in the *Gita* may be
classified into three disciplines, namely *Jnana Yoga* (the
path of knowledge), *Karma Yoga* (the path of action) and
Bhakti Yoga (the path of devotion). A practical philosophy
of life and means of attaining liberation are expounded upon
and a person may select one of the paths or may practice any
combination of the three.

THE PATH OF ACTION

The path of action or *Karma Yoga* is another essential doctrine of the *Bhagavad Gita*. In general, people live and work to economically prosper and to achieve personal goals and desires. In other words, actions are performed with strong motivations for success, recognition and achievement. Actions prompted by personal ends can often result in routineness, boredom, exhaustion, disappointment and failure. Attraction and repulsion, likes and dislikes, all are natural outcomes associated with actions carried out from the pragmatic point of view. According to the *Gita*, there is nothing wrong with working only for rewards and personal satisfaction, but such actions are, at most, only second best.

Action is the law of life because no one can exist, even for a moment, without carrying on some action. It is not only we humans who must work, for God has set Himself as an example of work for us to follow. Lord Krishna explains: "If I did not engage tirelessly in action, O Partha, men everywhere would follow My lead. If I should cease to work, these worlds would perish and I should be the cause of cosmic confusion and would destroy all these creatures" (3.23-24).

The main thrust of *Karma Yoga* is that one should develop renunciation in action but not renunciation of action. Ordinary works can be elevated to a higher plane when actions are carried out joyfully as a consecration. Then work ceases to be a burden and it becomes a sacred, loving sacrifice. Those who have risen above selfishness and dedicated their talents and energy to serving God and mankind, such as Albert Schweitzer, Mahatma Gandhi and Mother Teresa of Calcutta, have attained the purest form of action.

In this context, we can say that the power of the saints is far superior to the power of politicians. Saintly personalities carry on their work in a detached manner, without the thought of material rewards, whereas politicians are generally motivated by success, fame and fortune. Lord Krishna says: "He who perceives inaction in action, and action in inaction, is wise among men. He is a yogi and he performs all actions in a harmonious manner" (4.18). When action becomes a vocation, creativity flows naturally and the individual becomes simply a participant in the drama of life. Suffering and frustration cease when one rises above selfish interest.

This point naturally leads into a simple question. Is it possible not to get attached to action at all? The *Gita* emphatically points out that when an individual realizes the distinction between the self and the *gunas*, which operate within oneself, one does not get attached to action and its fruits. Once one recognizes that the modes of *sattva, rajas,* and *tamas* operate together to influence actions, one can free oneself from the results of actions, even while acting.

The ability to distinguish between the self and the *gunas* is possible only through the proper understanding of the *gunas*. Proper understanding provides insight into right and wrong actions and guides us in overcoming *rajasic* and *tamasic* influences, while increasing the *sattvic* influence upon actions. The *Gita* states: "Fixed in yoga . . . do your work, renouncing attachment and remaining even-minded in both success and failure" (2.48).

The *Gita* advocates that action should go beyond subjective motives and the forces of attraction and aversion. "To action alone you have a right and never to its fruits. Let not your motive be the fruits of action; nor let there be in you any attachment to inaction" (2.47). Every action should have the aim of upholding the highest good for the welfare of the world *(lokakalyana)*. Those who carry on work in this spirit are freed from both attraction and repulsion and the anxieties and sorrows of life.

As Lord Krishna says:

> Whatever you do, whatever you eat, whatever you offer, whatever you give away, whatever austerities you perform . . . do that as an offering to Me. Thereby you will be liberated from the bonds of action, which bear good and evil results. With your mind firmly set in the yoga of renunciation, you shall become free and come to Me (9.27-28).

This state of mind is only possible after one transcends selfishness and looks at good and bad fortune, gain and loss, victory and defeat, with equanimity, accepting it all as the will of God.

THE PATH OF KNOWLEDGE

Lord Krishna explains to Arjuna the nature of knowledge and the means to attain *Jnana Yoga* (right knowledge). The path of knowledge ultimately leads to the understanding of Brahman and the attainment of freedom in Brahman.

It is a commonly mistaken notion that the path of knowledge is reserved for intellectual aristocrats, but this path is open to all. "Even if you are the most sinful of all sinners, you shall cross over all evil by the raft of knowledge" (4.36). Brahman is the all-pervading power in this universe and resides in each person as *atman*. Therefore, man is primarily a spiritual being and the *summum bonum* of life is to realize Brahman within oneself.

Ordinary experiences are very limited in nature and distract one from the spiritual aspects of being. Empirical and scientific knowledge cannot lead one toward perfection and spiritual realization. The key which unlocks the door to the path of knowledge is *integral knowledge*, which transcends the limitations of the empirical and scientific realm.

The first impediment to gaining proper knowledge of the Self comes from the senses, so the control and mastery of the senses is an absolute necessity. To quote the *Gita*: "When a man broods over the sense objects, attachment to them arises. From attachment arises desire, and desire breeds anger. From anger comes delusion of mind, and from delusion, the loss of memory; from loss of memory, the destruction of discrimination; and from the destruction of discrimination, the man perishes" (2.62-2.63).

"The churning and restless senses . . . violently carry away the mind of even a wise man striving toward perfection" (2.60). That is why Lord Krishna advises: "Learn knowledge through humble reverence, through inquiry and through service. The wise seers who have perceived the Truth will teach you that knowledge" (4.34).

In the daily mundane transactions, one identifies strongly with all kinds of activities. Just as an actor masks his true identity when he plays different roles, likewise, the self identifies with its activities. John may say that he is a businessman, a fundraiser for the Republican Party, a country and western singer, and a volunteer worker with the mentally retarded. What John does defines his self image. But John's various activities do not lead him to an understanding of the true identity of his self. The real self is hidden beneath the labyrinth of outer identifications. As long as the individual identifies his consciousness with the events and roles played in his life, he can lead a moral and just life but he will never discover his inner self in its unalloyed state.

The way of knowledge requires certain preliminary preparations in the quest for self-realization, namely, the rejection of selfishness and passion, the quieting of the emotions, purity of spirit, and the striving to completely block off the mind and thoughts from the external world. "Know that the self is the rider in the chariot of the body. Understanding is the charioteer and the mind is the reins. The senses are the horses and worldly desires are the roads on which they run. . . . If the charioteer unwisely fails to restrain the mind, the senses run wild, like vicious horses. But if he wisely restrains the mind, then the senses are under control, like the good horses of a fine charioteer" (*Katha Up.* 3.3.6).

The primary method employed in the path of knowledge is *dhyana* (meditation). In *Jnana Yoga,* concentration techniques are practiced which silence the faculties, thereby shutting off sense impressions, emotions and thinking. The *Gita* counsels:

> Just as a lamp in a windless place does not flicker, similarly does the yogi of controlled mind practice concentration on the Self. . . . Giving up without exception all longings born of selfish will and completely taming the unruly senses with the mind; let him gain tranquility little by little. With a firm grip on reason and the mind abiding in the Self, let him not think of anything else (6.19-24).

Jnana Yoga is a hard path to travel. However, "those whose ignorance is destroyed by the knowledge of the Self find that knowledge illuminates the Supreme Self like the sun. With thought absorbed in That (the Supreme), with the self fixed on That, making That their whole aim, going toward That, they go the way that has no return, for their sins have been washed away by knowledge" (5.16-17). The inward experience of supreme consciousness, the highest state attainable in this body, is indeed the peak spiritual experience. That is why Lord Krishna says: "He who finds happiness within, joy within, inner radiance within, that yogi becomes Brahman and attains *Brahmanirvana* (freedom in Brahman)" (5.24).

THE PATH OF DEVOTION

In *Bhakti Yoga*, the cool contemplation of *Jnana Yoga* is replaced by hot devotion. This is the most universal of the three paths of self-realization or God realization. The path of devotion is open to all, rich or poor, educated or illiterate. The Lord says: "I am impartial toward all beings. There is none hateful or dear to Me. But those who worship Me with devotion are in Me and I am also in them" (9.29). The essence of devotion is prayer and prayer is the direct channel for communication with God. Lord Krishna instructs: "Fix your mind on Me, be devoted to Me, worship Me, bow down to Me. Thus having disciplined yourself, taking Me as the Supreme Goal, you shall come to Me" (9.34).

Bhakti Yoga is the most vital aspect of Hinduism and has kept Hinduism alive through the ages, in spite of the fact that there are no established, organized dogmas or fixed modes of worship. The rich symbols, rituals, and hundreds of images of God are all outward expressions of the devotion in the hearts of the worshippers. The vast array of symbols and images of God, as well as the manifold modes of worship in India, quite often baffle Westerners. But, for a Hindu, every form of worship done in good faith is a true path to God and salvation. Krishna promises, "In whatever way men take refuge in Me, I love them in that way. Men everywhere follow My path" (4.11).

The concept of a loving God predominates in the writings on the path of devotion. The Lord promises to protect and preserve those devotees who "worship Me, meditating upon Me with undivided heart," for "I bring what they lack and preserve what they already have" (9.22). Furthermore,

> He who has no hatred toward any creature; he who is friendly and compassionate, free from egotism and self pride, always content, self controlled and of firm resolve, with his mind and understanding dedicated to Me; he, My loving devotee, is dear to Me (12.13-14).

The followers of the path of devotion seek the ecstasy of communion with God and worship Him as the Lord and Master. What predominates is not theoretical meditation about God but the abundant love of God.

The only prerequisite to *Bhakti Yoga* is *sraddha* (faith), the spirit of letting go with absolute trust in God, for Lord Krishna says, "In whatever form a devotee seeks to worship Me with faith, in that form I sustain his unwavering faith" (7.21). However, "the ignorant one, who has no faith and is full of doubt, perishes. For he who doubts, there is neither this world, nor the world beyond, nor happiness" (4.40).

One may even stray from one's traditional *dharma* and

still attain salvation through this path. The Lord advises Arjuna to "abandon all *dharmas* and take refuge in Me alone. Do not grieve for I shall set you free from all sins" (18.66).

God responds to the devotee with love, mercy and forgiveness and showers His *prasada* (grace) on man because it is His very nature to do so. Both the virtuous and the sinners will be saved if they open up their hearts and seek the Lord. As Lord Krishna puts it:

> Even if a man of the most sinful conduct worships Me with singleminded devotion, he must be re- garded as righteous, for he has rightly resolved. Swiftly he becomes altogether righteous and attains everlasting peace. Know certainly . . . that My loving devotee never perishes (9.30-31).

In *Bhakti Yoga*, the devotee completely surrenders to God and finds *sharanagati* (final refuge) in Him. Faith, trust and refuge in God are not only a powerful antidote to existential anxiety, but also give comfort and peace in this life and *moksha* (salvation) in the next. The devotee will be released from the cycle of births and deaths, as Lord Krishna has promised: "Whosoever remembers Me alone at the hour of death, when he leaves his body and departs, comes into My state of being—of this there is no doubt" (8.5).

The essential teachings of the *Gita* and the three yogas point the way to perfection and liberation. Each person may choose the path which suits his or her temperament and needs to attain self-realization and freedom from *Samsara*.

THE
BHAGAVAD GITA

OTHER NAMES USED FOR
ARJUNA AND KRISHNA

Arjuna is referred to as: Best of the Bharatas
Bharata
best of men
Gudakesha
joy of the Kurus
lord of the Bharatas
mighty-armed one
Pandava
Partha
scorcher of the foe
sinless one
son of Kunti
winner of wealth

Krishna is referred to as: Blessed Lord
Govinda (herdsman)
Hrishikesha (bristling-haired one)
Imperishable One
Janardana (liberator of men)
Keshava (fine-haired one)
lotus-eyed One
Madhava (husband of Lakshmi)
Madhusudana (slayer of the demon Madhu)
mighty-armed One
slayer of foes
Supreme Lord
Supreme Person
Vasudeva (son of Vasudeva)
Vishnu

Chapter One

THE GRIEF
OF
ARJUNA

1 Dhritarashtra[1] said:
In the field of righteousness, the field[2] of the Kurus, what did my men[3] and the sons of Pandu[4] do, O Sanjaya, when they assembled together ready to fight?

2 Sanjaya[5] said:
Having seen the army of the Pandavas drawn up for the battle, King Duryodhana approached his teacher Drona[6] and spoke these words:

3 Behold, O master, this mighty army of the sons of Pandu arrayed by your intelligent disciple, the son of Drupada.[7]

4 Here on our side are heroes, powerful archers, in battle equal to Bhima[8] and Arjuna, Yuyudhana,[9] Virata[10] and King Drupada, a mighty warrior,

5 Dhrishtaketu[11] and Chekitana[12] and the heroic King of Kashi (Benares), Purujit and Kuntibhoja[13] and Shaibya,[14] all the best of men.

6 And powerful Yudhamanyu,[15] Uttamauja[16] the valiant, the son of Subhadra,[17] and the sons of Draupadi,[18] all excellent warriors indeed.

7 Also know, O best of the twice-born, the leaders of our own army. I will name those who are most distinguished that you may recognize them all.

8 Yourself and Bhishma[19] and Karna[20] and Kripa,[21] who is victorious in battle, Ashvatthama[22] and Vikarna,[23] Jayadratha and Somadatta's son.

9 And many other heroes are here who will risk their lives for me. All of them are armed with many weapons and all are well skilled in war.

10 Inadequate is this army of ours protected by Bhishma, while the army led by Bhima is indeed adequate for victory.

11 May you all, stationed firm in your respective positions, protect Bhishma on all fronts.

12 Bhishma, the elder Kuru, the valiant grandsire, roaring like a lion, loudly blew his conch shell, bringing joy to Duryodhana.

13 The conches and kettle drums, cymbals, trumpets and horns, all blared suddenly and the uproar was tremendous.

14 Thereupon, Krishna and Arjuna, standing in their magnificent chariot drawn by white horses, also blew their divine conches.

15 Krishna blew his conch Panchajanya and Arjuna his Devadatta; and Bhima, the doer of formidable deeds, blew his great conch Paundra.

16 King Yudhishthira, the son of Kunti, blew his conch Anantavijaya; and Nakula and Sahadeva[24] blew their Sughosha and Manipushpaka.

17 And the King of Kashi, the mighty archer, Shikandi the great warrior, Dhrishtadyumna[25] and Virata and Satyaki the invincible,

18 Drupada and the sons of Draupadi, and the strong-armed son of Subhadra, blew their own conches on all sides, O lord of the earth.

19 Resounding through earth and sky, that tumultuous uproar shook the hearts of the sons of Dhritarashtra.

20 Then seeing the sons of Dhritarashtra drawn up in battle array and the clash of arms about to begin, Arjuna, the son of Pandu whose banner bore the emblem of Hanuman, took up his bow,

21 And spoke these words to Hrishikesha: Drive my chariot between the two armies, O immovable one,

22 So that I may see clearly those who stand there desirous to fight and with whom I must fight in this strife of battle.

23 That I may see those who have come here ready to fight and eager to please the evil-minded son of Dhritarashtra.

24 Sanjaya said:
Thus requested by Gudakesha, Hrishikesha stationed that
fine chariot between the two armies, O Bharata.

25 Facing Bhishma and Drona and all the rulers of the earth,
he said: See, O Partha, all the Kurus gathered here.

26 Arjuna saw lined up in both armies, fathers, grandfathers,
teachers, maternal uncles, brothers, sons, grandsons and
companions;

27 Also fathers-in-law and the dear ones in both armies.
When the son of Kunti[26] saw all these kinsmen standing
on opposite sides,

28 He was overcome with tremendous compassion and grief,
and he sorrowfully spoke: Seeing my own people, O
Krishna, assembled here eager to fight,

29 My limbs fail, my mouth dries up, my body trembles and
my hair stands on end;

30 The bow Gandiva slips from my hand and my skin is
burning all over my body. I am unable to stand and my
mind is reeling.

31 I see bad omens, O Keshava, and I forsee no good in
slaughtering my own people in battle.

32 I desire neither victory, nor kingdom, nor even any
pleasures, O Krishna. Of what use is the kingdom to us,
O Govinda, or of what use are pleasures and even life
itself?

33 Those for whose sake we long for kingdom, luxuries and pleasures, are all standing here on the battlefield, risking their lives and riches.

34 Teachers, fathers, sons and grandfathers, uncles, fathers-in-law, grandsons, brothers-in-law, and other relatives,

35 These I do not want to kill even though they should kill me, O Madhusudana, not even for domination over the three worlds, how much less for just this earth!

36 What joy shall we find in killing the sons of Dhritarashtra, O Janardana? Sin will possess us if we kill these usurpers.

37 We ought not kill the sons of Dhritarashtra, our kinsmen. How can we be happy, O Madhava, by killing our own people?

38 Even if they, with their minds overcome by greed, see no evil in the destruction of families and see no sin in treachery to friends;

39 Why should we not have the conscience to turn back from such a sin, O Janardana, we who clearly see the evil in the destruction of the family?

40 In the destruction of the family, its ancient laws (*dharmas*) are destroyed, and when laws perish, lawlessness overtakes the entire family.

41 When lawlessness prevails, O Krishna, the women of the family become unchaste, and when the women become corrupt, there arises mixing of the castes, O Varshneya.

42 This mixing of the castes leads into hell for the family as
well as the destroyers of the family because the spirits of
their ancestors fall when deprived of the ceremonial
offerings.

43 By the sinful deeds of the destroyers of families, which
cause the mixing of the castes, the eternal laws of caste
and the family are destroyed.

44 Thus have we heard it said, O Janardana, that those
whose family laws (*dharmas*) are lost must dwell in hell.

45 Alas, we are set to commit a great sin; we have resolved
to kill our own kinsmen to satisfy our greed for the
kingdom and its pleasures.

46 It would be far better for me if the sons of Dhritarashtra,
weapons in hand, should kill me in battle, unarmed and
unresisting.

47 Sanjaya said:
Having spoken thus on the battlefield, his heart overcome
with grief, Arjuna sank down on his chariot seat and cast
aside his bow and arrow.

Chapter Two

THE PATH OF REALITY

1 Sanjaya said:
To him who was thus overwhelmed by compassion, whose troubled eyes were filled with tears, and who was depressed, Madhusudana spoke these words.

2 The Blessed Lord said:
Whence has come to you such faintheartedness in this hour of peril? It is unworthy of an Aryan,[1] it is dishonorable, it does not lead to heaven, O Arjuna.

3 Fall not into cowardly impotence, O Partha, for it does not befit you. Shake off this petty faintheartedness and arise, O scorcher of the foe.

4 Arjuna said:
But how, O Madhusudana, can I fight with arrows in battle against Bhishma and Drona, who are worthy of veneration, O slayer of foes?

5 It is better to live on alms in this world rather than to slay these honorable masters. By slaying these venerable masters, I would enjoy wealth and pleasures smeared with their blood.

6 Nor do we know which is better for us, whether we should conquer them or they should conquer us. The sons of Dhritarashtra are facing us here; we should not even wish to live after slaying them.

7 My very being is overwhelmed with the weakness of pity and my mind is puzzled about my duty (*dharma*).[2] I appeal to You to tell me which is better. Teach me, your disciple, who have taken refuge in You.

8 I do not indeed see what will dispel the grief which is drying up my senses, even if I should obtain a rich and unrivaled kingdom on earth or even lordship over the gods in heaven.

9 Sanjaya said:
Having thus spoken to Hrishikesha, the mighty Gudakesha said to Govinda, "I will not fight," and he became silent.

10 To him who was depressed in the midst of the two armies, O Bharata (Dhritarashtra), Hrishikesha, smilingly as it were, spoke these words.

11 The Blessed Lord said:
You have been grieving for those who should not be grieved for, yet you speak words about wisdom. The wise grieve neither for the living nor for the dead.

12 Never was there a time when I was not, nor you, nor these ruling princes. Never will there be a time hereafter when we all shall cease to be.

13 As the embodied Self[3] passes through childhood, youth and old age in this body, so does It pass into another body. The wise man is not bewildered by this.

14 O Son of Kunti, material sensations give rise to heat and cold, pain and pleasure. They are transient; they come and go. Bear them patiently, O Bharata.

15 The man who is not disturbed by these sensations, O best of men, who remains calm in pain and pleasure, who is wise, is able to attain immortality.

16 The Unreal never is, the Real[4] never ceases to be. This conclusion is perceived by the seers of truth.

17 Know that all by which this universe is pervaded is indestructible. No one can bring the annihilation of that which is immutable.

18 All these bodies of the eternal embodied soul, which is imperishable and incomprehensible, are said to have to come to an end. Therefore fight, O Bharata.

19 He who understands that this Self is a slayer, and he who understands that It is slain; neither of them have wisdom. The Self neither slays nor is slain.

20 It is never born, nor does It die at anytime; nor, having once been, will It again cease to be. It is unborn, eternal, permanent and primal. It is not slain when the body is slain.

21 He who knows the Self to be indestructible, eternal, unborn and immutable, how can that person, O Partha, slay anyone or cause another to slay?

22 Just as a person discards worn-out clothes and puts on new ones, so too the embodied Self casts off old and worn-out bodies and enters into other new ones.

23 Weapons cannot cut It; fire does not burn It; waters do not drench It; nor does the wind wither It.

24 It cannot be pierced; fire cannot burn It; nor can It be wetted or dried. It is eternal, all-pervading, unchanging, and immovable. It is the same forever.

25 It is said to be unmanifest, unthinkable and unchangeable. Therefore, knowing It as such, you should not grieve.

26 Moreover, even if you think that the Self is born and dies again and again, even then, O mighty-armed one, you should not grieve.

27 For one who is born, death is certain; and for one who is dead, birth is certain. So you should not grieve for what is inevitable.

28 Unmanifest are all beings in their beginning, O Bharata, manifest in their middle states, and unmanifest again in their ends. What is there to lament?

29 One looks upon the Self as a wonder, another speaks of It as a wonder, and another hears of It as a wonder; even after having heard, no one actually knows It.

30 The Self, which dwells in the body of everyone, O Bharata, is eternal and can never be slain.[5] Therefore, you should not grieve for any creature.

31 Moreover, after considering your own duty,[6] you should not waver. There is no greater good for a Kshatriya[7] than a battle fought for a just cause.

32 Happy are the Kshatriyas, O Partha, for whom such a battle has come on its own accord as a gateway to heaven.

33 Now, if you refuse to fight this righteous battle, then, by failing in your own duty and honor, you will incur sin.

34 People will recount forever your lasting dishonor. And for one who has been honored, dishonor is much worse than death.

35 The great warriors will believe that you have retreated from the battle out of fear and those who have thought highly of you will lose esteem for you.[8]

36 Your enemies will speak of you with ill will, slandering your manhood. Could anything be more miserable than that?

37 If you are killed, you will go to heaven; if victorious, you will enjoy the earth. Therefore, arise resolved to fight, O son of Kunti.

38 Treating alike pleasure and pain, gain and loss, victory and defeat, prepare yourself for battle. Thus you will incur no sin.

39 This is the wisdom (*buddhi*)[9] of the Sankhya[10] imparted to
you, O Partha. Now listen to the wisdom of the Yoga.
Disciplined by this thought, you will free yourself from
the bondage of works.

40 No effort is lost and no harm prevails in this path (of
Yoga). Even a little of this righteousness (*dharma*) saves
a man from great fear.

41 In this, O joy of the Kurus, there is only one earnest and
resolute understanding; but the thoughts of the irresolute
are many-branched and unending.

42–43 The unwise who delight in the letter of the Vedas and
say that there is nothing else, whose selves are filled with
desire, who are intent on heaven, utter flowery words and
lay down specific rites for the attainment of pleasure and
power, resulting in rebirth as the reward for their actions.

44 The discriminating intelligence is not set in self-
concentration for those who cling to pleasure and power
and whose minds are carried away by these words of the
Vedas.

45 The action of the three *gunas*[11] is the subject matter of the
Vedas. Be free, O Arjuna, from the three *gunas*; be free
from the dualities; be firmly fixed in goodness (*sattva*).
Do not care for acquisition of property or its preservation
and be established in the Self.

46 As much use as there is in a pond flooded with water on
every side, so much use is there in all the Vedas for an
enlightened seer who has knowledge.

47 To action alone you have a right and never to its fruits. Let not your motive be the fruits of action; nor let there be in you any attachment to inaction.

48 Fixed in yoga, O winner of wealth, do your work, renouncing attachment and remaining even-minded in both success and failure. This equanimity[12] of mind is called yoga.

49 Far inferior indeed is mere action, O winner of wealth, to action performed with the yoga of wisdom. Seek refuge in the yoga of wisdom. Pitiful are those who work for results.

50 He who has reached evenness of mind casts off both good and evil deeds in this life. Therefore strive for yoga, which is skill in action.

51 The wise who have attained evenness of mind renounce the fruits of action. The wise are freed from the fetters of birth and attain the state that is beyond sorrow.

52 When your mind has crossed the forest of delusion, you will become indifferent to what has been heard and what is yet to be heard.

53 When your mind, which is bewildered by the Vedic texts, stands firm and steady in the Self, then you shall attain yoga.

54 Arjuna said:
What is the description of the man of steadfast wisdom who is merged in concentration (*samadhi*), O Keshava? How does the man of steady wisdom speak, how does he sit, how does he walk?

55 The Blessed Lord said:
   When a man completely abandons all the desires of the
   heart, O Partha, and is satisfied in the Self by the Self
   alone, then he is called a man of steady wisdom.

56 He whose mind is untroubled by grief; he who has no
   longing for pleasures; he who is free from attachment,
   fear and rage; he is called a sage of steady wisdom.

57 He who is not attached to anything, who neither rejoices
   nor sorrows when he encounters good or evil, has his
   mind firmly set in wisdom.

58 When he completely withdraws the senses from the
   sense-objects, just as a tortoise draws in its limbs, then
   his mind is firmly fixed.

59 The objects of the senses disappear from the one who
   abstains from food, but the taste for them remains. But
   even the taste disappears from the one who has seen the
   Supreme.

60 The churning and restless senses, O son of Kunti, violently carry away the mind of even a wise man striving
   toward perfection.

61 Having brought them all under control, he should sit
   disciplined in yoga, focused on Me. He whose senses are
   under control has a steady mind.

62 When a man broods over the sense objects, attachment to
   them arises. From attachment arises desire, and desire
   breeds anger.

63 From anger comes delusion of mind, and from delusion, the loss of memory; from loss of memory, the destruction of discrimination;[13] and from the destruction of discrimination, the man perishes.

64 But a man of self-control, who moves in the world of the senses with his senses restrained, is free from attraction and aversion and thereby attains serenity of mind.

65 Through that serenity comes the cessation of all his sorrows. The intelligence of such a man of serene mind is soon grounded in peace.

66 There is no wisdom nor power of contemplation for the uncontrolled mind. Without contemplation, there is no peace; and without peace, how can there be happiness?

67 When the mind yields to the roving senses, it carries away one's discrimination just as a storm carries away a ship on the waters.

68 Therefore, O mighty-armed one, he whose senses are completely withdrawn from their objects has his wisdom firmly grounded.

69 In that which is night to all beings, the man of self-discipline is awake; that which is day to all other beings is night for the sage who sees.

70 No one who longs for desires attains peace but rather he into whom all desires merge like waters into the ocean, which ever being filled yet remains unmoved.

71 The man who abandons all desires and acts free from lust, indifferent to possessions and without egotism, attains peace.

72 This is the divine state, O Partha. Having attained it, one is no longer bewildered. Fixed in it, even at the hour of death, one attains liberation in Brahman.

Chapter Three

THE YOGA
OF
ACTION

1 Arjuna said:
  If you hold, O Janardana, that knowledge is superior to action, why then do you urge me, O Keshava, to do this violent deed?[1]

2 With these apparently perplexing words, You seem to confuse my understanding. Therefore, tell me definitely the one way by which I can reach the Supreme Good.

3 The Blessed Lord said:
  O sinless one, since the beginning, a twofold way has been taught by Me in this world; the path of knowledge for the contemplative and that of works for men of action.[2]

4 Not by abstention from works does a man attain freedom from action; nor by mere renunciation (of works) alone does he rise to perfection.

5 Indeed, no one can exist, even for a moment, without doing some action. Everyone is forced to work, helplessly driven by the forces born of nature.

6 He who restrains his senses, but continues remembering in his mind the pleasures of the senses, is deluded and is said to be a hypocrite.

7 But he who curbs his senses with the mind, O Arjuna, and then, free from attachment, directs his senses in the path of works (*karma yoga*), he is superior.

8 Do your allotted work, for action is indeed better than inaction and even the mere maintenance of your body is not possible without action.

9 This world is bound by action (*karma*), except for work done as a sacrifice. Therefore, O son of Kunti, do your work as a sacrifice[3] and become free from the bonds of desire.

10 In the beginning, Prajapati[4] created mankind together with sacrifice and said: "By this shall you multiply and it (Kamadhuk[5]) shall grant all your desires."

11 By this (sacrifice) may you cherish the gods and may the gods cherish you. Thus by cherishing each other, you shall attain the Supreme Good.

12 Cherished by your sacrifice, the gods will give you your desired pleasures. He is indeed a thief who enjoys their gifts without offering anything to them in return.

13 The good persons who eat what is left of the sacrifice are released from all sins;[6] but the wicked who cook food only for themselves verily eat sin.

14 From food creatures are born; from rain food is produced; from sacrifice rain comes into being; and sacrifice is born of work.

15 Know that action originates from Brahman, and Brahman springs from the imperishable. Therefore, the all-pervading Brahman is eternally established in sacrifice.

16 Here on earth, he who does not follow the wheel thus set in motion is evil in nature; by indulging in the senses, he lives in vain, O Partha.

17 He whose delight is in the Self alone, who is satisfied with the Self, who is content in the Self, for him no work remains to be done.

18 He who has nothing to gain by actions done in this world, nor anything to lose by actions not done, he is not dependent upon mortal creatures for any object.

19 Therefore, always perform without attachment the work that should be done. By doing work without attachment, man attains the Supreme.

20 Through the path of action alone, men like Janaka[7] and others reached perfection. You should perform action also with the intention of guiding the people in the right direction.[8]

21 Whatever a great man does, others will copy. The people will follow whatever standard he sets.

22 O Partha, there is no work which I need to accomplish in all the three worlds, nor is there anything which I have yet to gain; nevertheless, I am still engaged in action.

23 If I did not engage tirelessly in action, O Partha, men everywhere would follow My lead.

24 If I should cease to work, these worlds should perish and I should be the cause of cosmic confusion and would destroy all these creatures.

25 As the unwise act with attachment to their work, O Bharata, so should a wise man act without attachment for the good of the world.

26 Let no wise man create confusion in the minds of the ignorant who are attached to (selfish) action. He should, rather, inspire others to act by his disciplined performance of actions.

27 All kinds of actions[9] are done by the modes of nature but he whose mind is confused by egotism thinks, "I am the doer."

28 He who knows the true distinction between the soul and the modes of nature and their works, O mighty-armed, realizes that it is the modes which operate upon the modes, and he does not get attached.

29 Those who are deluded by the modes of nature become attached to the actions of the modes. However, let no one who understands this unsettle the ignorant, whose knowledge is imperfect.

30 Offering all your actions to Me, with your consciousness fixed on the universal Self, having become free from longing and selfishness, cast off your grief and fight!

31 Those men, full of faith and without murmuring, who steadfastly practice this teaching of Mine are also released from the bondage of actions.

32 But those who sneer at my teaching and do not follow it, know them to be blind to all wisdom, devoid of discrimination, and doomed to destruction.

33 Even the man of knowledge behaves according to his own nature. Beings follow their own nature. Of what use is restraint?

34 The attachment and aversion which the senses feel for their objects are seated (in the senses). Let no one come under the sway of these two,[10] for they are his enemies.

35 Better to perform one's own duty (*dharma*) imperfectly than to perform the duty of another perfectly. Better to carry out one's own duty, even unto death, for to follow another's duty is perilous.

36 Arjuna said:
Then, what makes a man commit sin unwillingly, as if driven by force, O Varshneya?

37 The Blessed Lord said:
It is selfish desire, it is anger, born of the mode of passion (*rajas*), all-consuming and most sinful. Know this to be the enemy here on earth.

38 As fire is wrapped by smoke, as a mirror is veiled by dust, as an embryo is enclosed by the womb, so too is knowledge obscured by passion.

39 Knowledge is clouded, O son of Kunti, by the insatiable fire of desire which is the constant enemy of the wise.

40 The senses, the mind and the intellect are said to be its seat. Through them, it clouds knowledge and misleads the embodied soul.

41 Therefore, O best of the Bharatas, control your senses first and kill this evil destroyer of insight and knowledge.

42 The senses, they say, are superior. Superior to the senses is the mind, superior to the mind is the intellect, and superior to the intellect is He.

43 Thus, knowing that which is higher than the intellect, control the self by the Self and destroy the enemy, O mighty-armed one, which comes in the form of desire and is difficult to conquer.

Chapter Four

THE YOGA
OF
KNOWLEDGE

1 The Blessed Lord said:
I proclaimed this eternal yoga to Vivasvat, Vivasvat revealed it to Manu, and Manu imparted it to Ikshvaku.

2 Thus it was handed down in succession; the royal seers knew it. But over a long span of time, this yoga was lost on earth, O scorcher of the foe.

3 Today, the same ancient yoga is taught to you by Me; for you are My devotee and friend and this secret is supreme indeed.

4 Arjuna said:
Later was your birth and far earlier was the birth of Vivasvat. How am I to understand that you are the one who imparted this yoga to him in the beginning?

5 The Blessed Lord said:
My past births are many, as are yours, O Arjuna. I know them all but you know them not, O scorcher of the foe.

6 Though I am unborn and imperishable, though I am the Lord of all creatures, yet by controlling my own nature, I come into being by My supernatural power (*maya*).[1]

7 Whenever there is a decline of righteousness (*dharma*) and the uprising of unrighteousness (*adharma*), O Bharata, then I incarnate Myself.

8 For the protection of the good, for the destruction of the wicked, and for the establishment of righteousness, I come into being from age to age.

9 He who thus perceives My birth and work as divine will not be born again when he leaves his body, rather, he will come to Me, O Arjuna.

10 Delivered from passion, fear and anger, immersed in Me, seeking refuge in Me alone, and purified by the fire of wisdom, many have become one with My being.

11 In whatever way men take refuge in Me, I love them in that way. Men everywhere follow My path, O Partha.

12 Those who desire success in their work on earth worship the gods here, for in this world of men success comes swiftly through works.

13 The four castes[2] were created by Me according to the divisions of qualities (*gunas*) and work (*karma*); although I am its creator, yet know Me to be beyond action or change.

14 Actions do not contaminate Me, nor do I yearn for the fruit of action. He who knows Me thus is not bound by his actions.

15 Knowing this, the ancients worked while seeking liberation. Therefore, do your work just as the ancients did earlier.

16 Even the sages are perplexed about what action is and what inaction is. Therefore, I will tell you what action is so that you may know and be delivered from evil.

17 One has to understand what action really is and what wrong action is. Likewise, one has to understand what inaction is. Complex to understand is the way of action.

18 He who perceives inaction in action, and action in inaction, is wise among men. He is a yogi and he performs all actions in a harmonious manner.

19 He whose undertakings are devoid of all desire and self-will, whose actions are burned up in the fire of knowledge, him the wise men call a sage.

20 Having given up all attachment to the fruits of action, ever content and free, although thoroughly wrapped up in work, in fact he does nothing at all.

21 Free from desires, with his body and mind under control, renouncing all possessions, and performing action with the body alone, he incurs no sin.

22 Content with whatever gain comes to him, transcending the dualities (of pleasure and pain), free from jealousy, and steady-minded in success and failure, even though engaging in action, he is not bound.

23 One who is free from attachment, who is liberated, whose thoughts rest in wisdom, who performs works as a sacrifice (*yagna*), all his *karma* is entirely dissolved.

24 Brahman is the offering and Brahman is the oblation. By Brahman it is offered into the (sacrificial) fire of Brahman. Brahman is to be attained by him who thus realizes Brahman in his actions.

25 Some yogis offer oblations to the gods, while others offer the self as sacrifice by the self into the fire of Brahman.

26 Others offer their senses like hearing and the other senses into the fires of restraint, while others offer sound and the other objects of the senses into the fires of the senses.

27 Yet others offer all the actions of the senses and all the functions of the life force (*prana*)[3] into the yoga of self-restraint, which is kindled by knowledge.

28 Likewise, some offer as sacrifice their wealth, their penance, or their practice of yoga; while others of disciplined mind and strict vows offer their scriptural learning and knowledge.

29 Some, who are devoted to the regulation of breath control (*pranayama*)[4], having restrained the movement of *prana* (inhalation) and *apana* (exhalation), offer as sacrifice *prana* into *apana* and *apana* into *prana*.

30 Still others, who have controlled their diet, offer life breaths into life breaths as sacrifice. All these are knowers of sacrifice and by sacrifice their sins have been cleansed.

31 Those who eat the sacred food remaining from sacrificial ceremonies attain to the eternal Brahman. This world is not for him who offers no sacrifice, how then the other world, O best of the Kurus?

32 Thus, different kinds of sacrifices are spread through the Vedic scriptures. Know them all to be born of action and you shall be released.

33 Knowledge as a sacrifice is superior to any material sacrifice, O scorcher of the foe. All actions without exception culminate in knowledge.

34 Learn knowledge through humble reverence, through inquiry and through service. The wise seers who have perceived the Truth will teach you that knowledge.

35 Then you shall not again fall into delusion, O Pandava. By this knowledge, you will see all beings without exception in your Self and in Me.

36 Even if you are the most sinful of all sinners, you shall cross over all evil by the raft of knowledge.

37 As the blazing fire turns fuel to ashes, O Arjuna, so does the fire of knowledge turn all works to ashes.

38 There is nothing in the world equal in purity to knowledge. He who is perfected in yoga realizes it within his own heart in due time.

39 He who is full of faith and absorbed in knowledge, having restrained his senses, gains knowledge. Having gained knowledge, he soon attains the Supreme peace.

40 But the ignorant one, who has no faith and is full of
    doubt, perishes. For he who doubts, there is neither this
    world, nor the world beyond, nor happiness.

41 Works do not bind one who has renounced all actions
    through yoga, whose doubts are destroyed by knowledge,
    and who is poised in the self, O winner of wealth.

42 Therefore, having cut asunder with the sword of knowl-
    edge this doubt lingering in your heart, which is born of
    ignorance, resort to yoga and arise, O Bharata.

Chapter Five

THE YOGA
OF
RENUNCIATION

1 Arjuna said:
You commend, O Krishna, the renunciation of action and you also praise yoga. Tell me definitely which is the better of the two.

2 The Blessed Lord said:
Both renunciation and the yoga of action lead to the supreme good. But of these two, performance of action is superior to the renunciation of action.

3 He who neither hates nor desires is to be known as the everlasting renouncer (*sanyasi*); for, free from the dualities, O mighty-armed one, he is easily liberated from bondage.

4 The immature, not the wise, speak of the path of knowledge and the path of action as distinct from each other. He who has perfectly mastered one of them finds the fruit of both.

5 The goal reached by men of renunciation is reached by men of action also. He who sees that the way of renunciation and the way of action are one—he indeed sees!

6 True renunciation is hard to accomplish without the practice of yoga, O mighty-armed one; the sage who is disciplined in the yoga of action quickly reaches Brahman.

7 He who is devoted to the path of action and is pure in mind, who is master of his self and who has conquered his senses, whose self has become the Self in all beings, he is not tainted even though he acts.

8–9 "I am not doing anything at all," so thinks the yogi, the knower of Truth; for in seeing, hearing, touching, smelling, eating, walking, sleeping, breathing, and in speaking, emptying, grasping, opening and closing the eyes, he believes that the senses are only operating upon the sense objects.

10 He who works, abandoning attachment and resigning his actions to Brahman, is untouched by sin, just as a lotus petal is untouched by muddy water.

11 Having renounced attachment, the yogis perform action with only the body, the mind, the understanding or even merely the senses, for the purification of the self.

12 He who is disciplined in yoga, having abandoned the fruit of action, attains ultimate peace. But the undisciplined person, prompted by desire, is attached to the fruit of action and is therefore bound.

13 The embodied soul, who has mastered the senses and has renounced all actions with the mind, dwells happily in the nine-gated city, neither acting nor causing action to be done.

14 The all-pervading Lord does not create action or the means of action for the people nor the union of action with its fruits. Rather, nature works this out.

15 Nor does the all-pervading Lord partake in anyone's sin or merit. When knowledge is enveloped by ignorance, people are confused.

16 But those whose ignorance is destroyed by the knowledge of the Self find that knowledge illuminates the Supreme Self like the sun.

17 With thought absorbed in That (the Supreme), with the self fixed on That, making That their whole aim, going toward That, they go the way that has no return, for their sins have been washed away by knowledge.

18 The wise see no difference between a learned and humble Brahmin, a cow, an elephant, a dog, or even an outcaste.

19 Even in this world, rebirth is conquered by those whose minds are firmly set in impartiality. Brahman is without flaw and is the same in all. Therefore, they rest in Brahman.

20 Steadfast in his mind and undeluded, he who knows Brahman abides in Brahman. He does not rejoice when experiencing pleasure nor is he perturbed when experiencing pain.

21 He whose self is not attached to the external sense impressions finds happiness in the Self; his heart is one with Brahman through contemplation and he enjoys everlasting bliss.

22 The pleasures that are born of contact with objects are only sources of pain; they have a beginning and an end, O son of Kunti. The wise find no delight in them.

23 He who is able to withstand the upsurge of desire and anger here on earth, before he is liberated from the body, is indeed a yogi. He is a happy man.

24 He who finds happiness within, joy within, inner radiance within, that yogi becomes Brahman and attains freedom in Brahman (*Brahmanirvana*).

25 The sages whose sins have been destroyed, whose doubts have been resolved, who have mastered themselves, and who are dedicated in doing good to all creatures, attain freedom in Brahman (*Brahmanirvana*).

26 For the austere men (*yatis*), who are delivered from lust and wrath, who have controlled their thoughts and who have realized the Self, the bliss of Brahman lies close at hand.

27–28 Shutting out all outside contacts, fixing the gaze between the eyebrows, inhaling and exhaling evenly within the nostrils, having controlled the senses, the mind and understanding; the sage, who is devoted to liberation as his highest goal, who has cast away desire, fear and anger, is forever liberated.

29 Having known Me as the Lord of sacrifices and austerities, the mighty Lord of all the worlds, the Friend of all beings, he attains peace.

Chapter Six

THE YOGA
OF
MEDITATION

1 The Blessed Lord said:
He who performs ritual action which ought to be done without seeking its fruit is a true renouncer and a yogi; not he who fails to light the sacred fire and fails to perform the ritual acts.

2 Know that yoga is that which is called renunciation, O Pandava; for no one becomes a yogi without renouncing his heart's desires.[1]

3 For the sage who seeks to attain yoga, work is said to be the means. When he has attained yoga, peace is said to be the means.

4 When a man is attached neither to the sense-objects nor to works, and when he has renounced all the desires of the heart, then he is said to have attained yoga.

5 Let a man raise himself by the Self, let him not degrade himself; for the Self alone is the friend of the self and the Self alone is the enemy of the self.

6 The self is the friend of the Self for one who has conquered his self by the Self; but for one who has not conquered himself, his own self is hostile, like an enemy.

7 He who has conquered himself and is peaceful, who is absorbed in the Supreme Self, is ever steadfast in heat and cold, pleasure and pain, honor and dishonor.

8 He who is content with wisdom and knowledge, who is firm and self-poised, who has mastered his senses, to whom a lump of clay, a stone or a piece of gold are alike, is said to be a steadfast yogi of true discipline.

9 One excels among men who has equal regard for friends, companions, enemies, the impartial, the malicious, relatives, saints and sinners.

10 Let the yogi at all times strive to concentrate his mind on the Supreme Self, remaining alone in solitude, self-controlled and free from desires and possessions.

11 Establishing a firm seat for himself in a clean place that is neither too high nor too low and covered with sacred grass, a deerskin and a cloth, one over the other;

12 Sitting there, concentrating his mind on a single object, controlling his thought and the activity of the senses, let him practice yoga for self-purification.

13 Sitting still, holding the body, head and neck erect, firmly and steadily gazing at the tip of his own nose, without looking anywhere else;

14 Serene and fearless, faithful to the vow of celibacy, and in control of the mind, let him sit harmonized with his thoughts fixed on Me and devoted to Me.

15 Thus continually disciplining himself, with his mind and emotions well-controlled, the yogi attains to the supreme peace and joy abiding in Me, culminating in *nirvana*.

16 Yoga is not possible for him who eats too much, O Arjuna, nor for him who refrains from eating altogether. It is not for him who sleeps too much or too little.

17 For the man who is temperate in food and play, who is disciplined in his performance of actions, whose sleep and waking are regulated, for such a man yoga dispels all sorrow.

18 When the man of restrained mind is absorbed in the Self alone, free from the craving for desires, then he is said to be disciplined in yoga.

19 Just as a lamp in a windless place does not flicker, similarly does the yogi of controlled mind practice concentration on the Self.

20 Where thought enters into silence, stilled by the practice of concentration, one sees the Self through the self and is satisfied in the Self.

21 When he experiences that supreme happiness, which is perceived by the intelligence and transcends the senses, when once established in that, he does not depart from the truth.

22 Having attained this, he regards no other gain as greater; wherein established, he is not shaken even by profound sorrow.

23 Let yoga be known as the dissolution from the union with sorrow. This yoga should be practiced with firm determination and indomitable heart.

24 Giving up without exception all longings born of selfish will and completely taming the unruly senses with the mind.

25 Let him gain tranquility little by little. With a firm grip on reason and the mind abiding in the Self, let him not think of anything else.

26 No matter what causes his wavering and unstable mind to wander, let him restrain it and bring it under the control of the Self alone.

27 Supreme bliss comes to the yogi whose mind is peaceful, whose passions are calmed, who is free from sin and has become one with Brahman.

28 Freed from all sins, the yogi who steadfastly disciplines himself joyfully experiences the infinitely blissful touch of Brahman.[2]

29 He whose self is disciplined by yoga sees the Self present in all beings and all beings present in the Self; he sees the same self everywhere.

30 For him who sees Me everywhere and sees everything in Me, I am not lost to him and he is not lost to Me.

31 The yogi who is established in oneness worships Me as abiding in all beings; he dwells in Me, whatever his mode of living.

32 He who sees oneness everywhere, both in joy and in sorrow, who sees all as the image of his own self, he is the one whom I deem to be the supreme yogi, O Arjuna.

33 Arjuna said:
O Madhusudana, you have declared this yoga to be characterized by equanimity of mind. But I see no stable foundation for it because of the restlessness of the mind.

34 For the mind indeed is restless, O Krishna; it is turbulent, strong and obstinate. Restraining it is as difficult, I think, as restraining the wind.

35 The Blessed Lord said:
The fickle mind is no doubt restless and difficult to control, O mighty Arjuna, but by constant practice and detachment from worldly objects, it can be restrained, O son of Kunti.

36 I agree that yoga is hard to attain for one whose self is uncontrolled; however, it can be attained through proper means by the one who strives with self-control.

37 Arjuna said:
If one is endowed with complete faith but is unable to control himself, if his mind has wandered away from yoga, O Krishna, what direction should he take, having failed to attain perfection in yoga?

38 Does he not perish like a dispersing cloud, having fallen from both worlds (here and hereafter), unsteady and bewildered in the path of Brahman, O mighty Krishna?

39 Completely wipe out this doubt of mine, O Krishna, for no one but You can solve such a doubt.

40 The Blessed Lord said:
O Partha, neither here on earth nor in heaven is there any destruction for him; for no one who does good, dear friend, ends up in grief.

41 Having reached the worlds of the righteous and having lived there for a number of years, the man who has fallen away from yoga is born into the home of the holy and prosperous;

42 Or indeed he may be born into the family of wise yogis, for such a birth is very difficult to attain in this world.

43 There he regains the knowledge that he had acquired in his previous life and he strives even harder for perfection, O son of the Kurus.

44 Even against his own will, he is carried on irresistibly by his former effort. Even he who merely wishes to know of yoga rises beyond those who perform Vedic rites.

45 But the yogi who strenuously strives is completely cleansed of all sins, thereby becoming perfect through many births and reaching the ultimate goal.

46 The yogi is deemed to be greater than the ascetic, greater than the man of knowledge, and greater than the man of ritual action. Therefore, O Arjuna, become a yogi.

47 And of all yogis, the one who worships Me full of faith, with his inner self abiding in Me, him I hold to be the most devoted to me in yoga.

Chapter Seven

KNOWLEDGE AND EXPERIENCE

1 The Blessed Lord said:
 With your mind absorbed in Me, O Partha, taking refuge
 in Me and practicing yoga, hear how you shall know Me
 entirely, without any doubt.

2 I shall teach you in full this knowledge and wisdom; when
 once understood, nothing more remains to be known in
 this world.

3 Among thousands of people, hardly one strives for perfection; and even among those who strive and succeed,
 scarcely one knows Me in truth.

4 My material nature is eightfold:[1] earth, water, fire, air,
 ether, mind, reason and ego.

5 This is My lower nature, but also learn of My higher
 nature, O mighty-armed one, which is the indwelling
 spirit by which this world is sustained.

6 Realize that all beings are born from these two. I am the origin of the entire universe and also its dissolution.

7 Nothing higher than Me exists, O winner of wealth. Everything in this universe is strung on Me like pearls on a thread.

8 In water I am the taste, O son of Kunti; in the sun and moon I am the radiance; in all the Vedas I am the sacred syllable *Om*, in ether the sound, and in men their manliness.

9 In earth I am the pure fragrance and in fire I am the brightness. I am the life in all beings and the austerity in ascetics.

10 Know Me to be the eternal seed of all beings, O Partha. I am the intelligence of the intelligent and the splendor of the splendid.

11 I am the might of the mighty devoid of lust and passion. I am the desire in all beings which is in accordance with righteousness (*dharma*), O lord of the Bharatas.

12 And whatever states of being there may be, whether harmonious (*sattvic*), passionate (*rajasic*), or slothful (*tamasic*), know that they all stem from Me alone. I am not in them but they are in Me.[2]

13 Deluded by these three modes of nature, the whole world fails to recognize Me, who am eternal and above them (the modes of nature).

14 Divine indeed is My illusion (*maya*), consisting of the modes (*gunas*), which is hard to escape. Only those who take refuge in Me alone transcend this illusion.

15 Evildoers, the deluded and men of low mentality do not seek refuge in Me. Their minds are carried away by illusion and they are attached to demonic ways.

16 Four types of virtuous men worship Me, O Arjuna: the man in distress, the seeker of knowledge, the seeker of wealth, and the man of wisdom, O lord of the Bharatas.

17 Among them, the wise one stands out ever steadfast, worshipping Me alone. I am extremely dear to him and he is dear to Me.

18 Noble indeed are all these but the man of wisdom I regard to be My very Self; for he steadfastly trusts in Me alone as his highest goal.

19 The man of wisdom attains to Me after many births, realizing that "the Supreme (*Vasudeva*) is all." Such a great soul is very hard to find.

20 But those whose prudence has been lead astray by various desires resort to other gods and perform different rituals, constrained by their own natures.

21 In whatever form a devotee seeks to worship Me with faith, in that form I sustain his unwavering faith.

22 Endowed with that faith, he aspires to propitiate that god and from that god he obtains his desires; but, in fact, his desires are granted by Me alone.

23 The reward gained by these men of small minds is temporary. He who worships the gods goes to the gods, but My followers come to Me.

24 The unenlightened think of Me, the unmanifest, as possessing a manifest form. They are not aware of My higher nature, which is imperishable and supreme.

25 Veiled by My power of illusion, I am not revealed to all. This bewildered world knows Me not as the unborn and everlasting.

26 O Arjuna, I know all beings of the past, the present, and the future, but no one knows Me.

27 All beings in this world are born to delusion, O Bharata, and are overcome by the dualities arising from desire and hatred, O conqueror of foes.

28 But those mortals of virtuous deeds in whom sin has come to an end, whose actions are pure, and who are freed from the delusion of dualities, worship Me with firm vows.

29 Those who strive for deliverance from old age and death by taking refuge in Me, they thoroughly know Brahman, the Self (*Adhyatma*), and all about action.

30 Those who know Me as the Supreme Being, as the highest divinity, and as the highest sacrifice, they truly know Me with steadfast mind, even at the hour of death.

Chapter Eight

THE WAY
TO THE
ETERNAL BRAHMAN

1 Arjuna said:
What is Brahman? What is the individual self? What is karma? What is it that is said to underlie all the material elements? What is it that is said to underlie all the gods, O Supreme Person?

2 In what manner are all sacrifices sustained here in this body, O Madhusudana? And how are you to be known by the self-controlled persons at the hour of death?

3 The Blessed Lord said:
Brahman is the Imperishable, the Supreme. One's essential nature is called the individual self.[1] The creative power which brings beings into existence is known by the name *karma*.

4 The basis of all material elements is of perishable nature, the basis of all divine elements is the cosmic spirit (*Purusha*),[2] and I am the basis of all sacrifice here in the body, O best of the embodied.

5 And whosoever remembers Me alone at the hour of death, when he leaves his body and departs, comes into My state of being—of this there is no doubt.

6 Whatever state of being one thinks of while leaving his body at the time of death, he goes into that state of being,[3] O son of Kunti, and is ever absorbed in that state.

7 Therefore, think of Me at all times and fight. With your mind and spirit set on Me alone, you shall definitely come to Me.

8 He who is disciplined by the practice of yoga, who meditates on the Supreme and does not turn his mind to anything else, reaches the resplendent Spirit (*Purusha*), O Partha.

9 He who meditates on the ancient seer, the ruler, who is smaller than the atom, who is the supporter of all, whose form is incomprehensible, and who is bright like the sun, beyond the darkness;

10 He who meditates at the hour of death, with a steady mind filled with devotion and the strength of yoga, setting his vital breath (*prana*) between his eyebrows, he reaches the resplendent Supreme Person.

11 I shall briefly describe to you that state which the knowers of the Vedas call the Imperishable, into which the ascetics freed from passion enter, and desiring which they follow a life of self-control.

12–13 By firmly controlling all the avenues of the senses, by confining the mind within the heart,[4] and by drawing the life force into the head, he who is well-established in the practice of yoga, uttering the syllable "Om" which is Brahman, and meditating on Me as he departs, giving up his body, he goes to the Supreme Goal.

14 I am easy to reach for the yogi who is ever disciplined and who meditates on Me constantly with no other thoughts, O Partha.

15 Having come to Me and having reached the highest perfection, these great souls are no more subject to rebirth, which is transitory and an abode of pain.

16 From the realm of Brahma downward, the dwellers in all the worlds are subject to successive births, O Arjuna, but those who reach Me are not born again, O son of Kunti.

17 Those who know that the day of Brahma lasts thousands of eons,[5] and that the night of Brahma ends only after thousands of eons, they are the knowers of night and day.

18 At the dawn of the day, all manifestations are born from the unmanifest; and at nightfall, they dissolve again into that which is called the unmanifest.

19 The same multitude of beings, coming into existence again and again, are dissolved helplessly at nightfall, O Partha, and come into existence again at the dawn of the day.

20 But beyond the unmanifest, there is yet another unmanifest Eternal Being, who does not perish even when all beings perish.

21 This unmanifest (Being) is called the Imperishable (*Akshara*). This they call the Supreme Goal; having attained It, they return not again. That is My supreme abode.

22 This is the Supreme Person, attainable through undivided devotion, within whom all beings dwell and by whom the entire universe is pervaded, O Partha.

23 I will tell you, O best of the Bharatas, the time in which the yogis depart and do not return and also the time in which they depart and do return.

24 When they depart life by fire, by sunshine, by day, in the bright lunar fortnight, and during the six months of the northern solstice, the knowers of Brahman go to Brahman.

25 When departing by smoke, by night, in the dark fortnight and during the six months of the southern solstice of the sun, the yogi obtains lunar light and returns again.

26 These two paths—light and darkness—are thought to be the world's eternal paths. By the one, a man does not return, by the other, he is born again.

27 Knowing these two paths, O Partha, the yogi is not at all confused. Therefore, O Arjuna, be firm in yoga at all times.

28 The yogi who knows this transcends the fruits of action which are prescribed in the Vedas, in sacrifices, in austerities, and in gifts, and he reaches the supreme primal Abode.

Chapter Nine

THE YOGA
OF
MYSTICISM

1 The Blessed Lord said:
   To you, who do not disbelieve, I shall declare this most
   profound secret of wisdom accompanied by knowledge
   and discrimination. Once having learned this, you shall
   be released from evil.

2 This is the royal knowledge[1], the royal secret, the supreme purifier, which is known by direct experience,
   conforms to *dharma*, is easy to practice and imperishable.

3 Men who have no faith in this *dharma* fail to reach Me, O
   scorcher of the foe; rather, they return to the path of the
   cycle of birth and death (*samsara*).

4 This whole universe is pervaded by Me in My unmanifest
   form. All beings exist in Me but I do not exist in them.

5 And yet, beings do not exist in Me; behold My majestic
   power! My spirit which is the source and sustainer of all
   beings does not exist in them.

6 Just as the mighty wind that blows everywhere rests in the ether (*akasha*), likewise, know that all beings rest in Me.

7 All beings enter into My material nature (*Prakriti*) at the end of every cycle (*kalpa*), O son of Kunti, and at the beginning of every cycle, I create them again.

8 Controlling My own material nature, I create again and again this entire multitude of beings which are powerless under the sway of My material nature.

9 And these actions do not bind Me, O conqueror of wealth. I am seated above them as if unconcerned and detached from all this.

10 Under My supervision, material nature gives birth to all things, animate and inanimate; and for this reason, O son of Kunti, the universe revolves.

11 Not knowing My higher nature as the Supreme Lord of all beings, the deluded disregard Me when I assume a human form;

12 Being devoid of judgment and clinging to the deceptive nature of fiends and demons,[2] all their hopes, their actions, and their knowledge are in vain.

13 But the great souls abiding in the divine nature, O Partha, worship Me singlemindedly, knowing Me as the eternal source of all beings.

14 Ever glorifying Me and striving with firm resolve, bowing before Me in adoration, they worship Me devoutly.

15 Others, offering the oblation of knowledge, worship Me as the one or as the distinct or as the many, facing in all directions.

16 I am the ritual, I am the sacrifice, I am the oblation to the ancestors, I am the medicinal herb, I am the sacred chant, I am the clarified butter, and I am both the fire and the offering.

17 I am the father of this universe, the mother, the guardian, the grandfather, the object of knowledge, the purifier, the sacred syllable *Om*. I am also the Rik, the Sama, and the Yajus.[3]

18 I am the way, the sustainer, the lord, the witness, the abode, the refuge, and the loving friend. I am the origin, the dissolution, the ground, the treasure house, and the imperishable seed.

19 I radiate heat; I withhold and send forth rain; I am both immortality and death. I am being as well as non-being, O Arjuna.

20 Those who are knowledgeable in the three Vedas, who drink the soma juice and are cleansed from sin, worship Me with sacrifices and pray to go to heaven. They reach the holy world of Indra and enjoy the celestial pleasures of the gods.

21 Having enjoyed that heavenly world, they return to the world of mortals when their merit is exhausted. Thus adhering to the laws of the three Vedas and desiring enjoyment, they obtain the cycle of birth and death.

22 To those who worship Me, meditating upon Me with undivided heart, I bring what they lack and preserve what they already have.

23 Even those who worship other deities with love and faith worship Me alone, O son of Kunti, though not according to the law.

24 For I am the enjoyer and the lord of all sacrifices. But these men do not know Me in truth and so they fall.

25 Those who worship the gods go to the gods, those who worship the ancestors go to the ancestors, those who are devoted to the spirits go to the spirits, and those who worship Me will come to Me.

26 He who devotedly offers to Me a leaf, a flower, a fruit or water, that offering of love I accept from the pure of heart.

27 Whatever you do, whatever you eat, whatever you offer, whatever you give away, whatever austerities you perform, O son of Kunti, do that as an offering to Me.

28 Thereby you will be liberated from the bonds of action, which bear good or evil results. With your mind firmly set in the yoga of renunciation, you shall become free and come to Me.

29 I am impartial toward all beings. There is none hateful or dear to Me. But those who worship Me with devotion are in Me and I am also in them.

30 Even if a man of the most sinful conduct worships Me with single-minded devotion, he must be regarded as righteous, for he has rightly resolved.

31 Swiftly he becomes altogether righteous and attains everlasting peace. Know certainly, O son of Kunti, that My loving devotee never perishes.

32 For those who take refuge in Me, O Partha, even those born of low origin—including women, Vaishyas and Shudras⁴—also attain the supreme goal.

33 How much more then, the holy Brahmins and the devoted royal seers! Having entered into this impermanent and joyless world, devote yourself to Me.

34 Fix your mind on Me, be devoted to Me, worship Me, bow down to Me. Thus having disciplined yourself, taking Me as the Supreme Goal, you shall come to Me.

Chapter Ten

THE
DIVINE
MANIFESTATIONS

1 The Blessed Lord said:
Once more, O mighty-armed one, listen to My supreme word. Because you take delight in My words, I shall speak to you, desiring your well-being.

2 Neither the hosts of gods nor the great seers know My origin. In reality, I am the source of the gods and the great seers.

3 He who knows Me as the unborn, the beginningless, the mighty Lord of the world, is undeluded among mortals and is liberated from all sins.

4–5 Intelligence, knowledge, freedom from delusion, patience, truth, self-control, tranquility, pleasure and pain, birth and death, fear and fearlessness, non-violence, equanimity, contentment, austerity, charity, fame and dishonor, all these different qualities of beings arise from Me alone.

6 The seven great sages of ancient times, as well as the four Manus,[1] are of My nature and were born from My mind. From them, all these creatures in the world have originated.

7 He who truly knows My manifested lordship and power is united with Me by unwavering devotion, of this there is no doubt.

8 I am the source of everything, from Me everything evolves. Knowing this, the wise worship Me, endowed with faith.

9 With their hearts set on Me, their whole lives given to Me, enlightening one another and always speaking of Me, the wise find contentment and delight.

10 To those who are constantly devoted to Me and worship Me with love, I grant the yoga of discrimination[2] by which they come to Me.

11 Out of compassion for them, I who reside in their hearts destroy the darkness born of ignorance with the shining lamp of wisdom.

12 Arjuna said:
You are the supreme Brahman, the Supreme Abode, the Supreme Purifier, the everlasting Divine Spirit, the Primal God, the unborn and all-pervading Lord.

13 All the sages have declared this, the divine seers Narada, Asita, Devala and Vyasa. So also You have told me.

14 All that You have told me I believe to be true, O Keshava. For neither the gods nor the demons know Your manifestations, O Lord.[3]

15 You know Yourself through Yourself alone, O Supreme Person, O Creator of beings, O Lord of mankind, O God of gods, O Lord of the universe.

16 Please describe to me completely Your divine manifestations, by which You pervade these worlds and abide in them.

17 How may I know You, O Yogi, by constant meditation? In what forms are you to be thought of by Me, O Blessed Lord?

18 Explain to me once more in detail Your power and manifestation, O Janardana. For I can never be satiated with hearing Your nectar-like words.

19 The Blessed Lord said:
I will narrate to you My divine manifestations, but only those that are prominent. O best of the Kurus, for my manifestations are endless.

20 O Gudakesha, I am the self dwelling in the heart of all beings. I am the beginning, the middle and also the end of all beings.

21 Of the Adityas[4] I am Vishnu; of lights I am the radiant sun; of the Maruts[5] I am the Marichi and of the stars I am the moon.

22 Of the Vedas I am the Sama Veda;[6] of the gods I am Indra; of the senses I am the mind; and of the living beings I am consciousness.

23 Of the Rudras[7] I am Shiva; of the Yakshas and Rakshasas[8] I am Kubera[9]; of the Vasus[10] I am Agni[11]; and of the mountains I am Meru.

24 Of houshold priests, O Partha, know Me to be the chief Brihaspati;[12] of the military generals I am Skanda;[13] of waters I am the ocean.

25 Of the great seers I am Bhrigu; of words I am the sacred syllable *Om*; of sacrifices I am the silent prayer; and of immovable things I am the Himalaya.

26 Of all trees I am the sacred fig tree (*Ashvattha*); of the divine seers I am Narada; of the Gandharvas[14] I am Chitraratha; and of the perfected ones[15] I am Kapila the sage.

27 Of horses know Me to be Ucchaisravas, born of Amrita; of princely elephants I am Airavata; and of men I am the ruler;

28 Of weapons I am the thunderbolt; of cows I am Kamadhuk; of the procreators I am Kandarpa;[16] of the serpents I am Vasuki.[17]

29 Of the Nagas[18] I am Ananta; of the water creatures I am Varuna; of the ancestors I am Aryama; and of the enforcers of law and order I am Yama.[19]

30 Of the titans I am Prahlada; of measures I am time; of beasts I am the lion; and of birds I am Garuda.[20]

31 Of purifiers I am the wind; of warriors I am Rama;[21] of fishes I am the shark; and of rivers I am the Ganges.

32 Of creations, I am the beginning, the middle and the end, O Arjuna. Of sciences, I am the science of the Supreme Self; and of those who debate, I am reason.

33 Of letters I am the letter "A" and of compound words I am the *Dvandva*.[22] I am also the infinite time and the creator facing everywhere.

34 I am all-consuming death and I am the source of all beings that are yet to be born; and of the feminine qualities, I am fame, fortune, speech, memory, wisdom, courage and patience.

35 Of the Saman hymns, I am the Brihatsaman;[23] of meters I am the Gayatri;[24] of months I am Margashirsha;[25] and of seasons I am the flowering spring.

36 Of the gambler I am the gambling; of the splendid I am the splendor; I am victory, I am effort, and I am the goodness of the good.

37 Of the Vrishnis[26] I am Vasudeva;[27] of the Pandavas I am Dhananjaya; of the sages I am Vyasa;[28] and of poets, Ushana.

38 Of rulers I am the power; of those desirous of victory I am the guidance; of secret things I am the silence; and of the wise I am the wisdom.

39 And that which is the seed of all beings, that am I, O Arjuna; nor is there any being, moving or unmoving, that can exist without Me.

40 There is no end to My divine manifestations, O scorcher of the foe. I have told you this to illustrate My manifold forms.

41 Whatever being is glorious, prosperous or powerful, recognize it to have sprung from a spark of My splendor.

42 But what necessity is there for you to acquire such extensive knowledge, O Arjuna? I support the entire universe with a mere fragment of Myself.

Chapter Eleven

THE VISION
OF THE
UNIVERSAL FORM

1 Arjuna said:
Out of compassion for me, You have spoken about the ultimate mystery of the Self and my delusion has vanished by Your words.

2 I have heard from You in detail of the origin and the dissolution of beings, O lotus-eyed One, and also of Your indestructible greatness.

3 As You have declared Yourself to be, O Supreme Lord, even so it is. I long to see Your divine form, O Supreme Person.

4 O Lord, if you think that I shall be able to see this, then, O Master of yoga, reveal Your imperishable Self to me.

5 The Blessed Lord said:
O Partha, behold My forms, by the hundreds and thousands, of various kinds, divine and in a multitude of colors and shapes.

6 Behold the Adityas, the Vasus, the Rudras, the two
   Ashwins, and the Maruts. Behold many wonders that
   have never been seen before, O Bharata!

7 Behold now the entire universe, with everything moving
   and unmoving centered in My body, O Gudakesha, and
   whatever else you desire to see.

8 You cannot see Me with your human eye. I will give you
   divine sight. Behold My majestic power.

9 Sanjaya said:
   Having thus spoken, O King,[1] the great Lord of yoga,
   Hari, revealed to Partha His majestic divine form.

10 With many mouths and eyes, with many wondrous
   aspects, with many divine ornaments, with many divine
   uplifted weapons;

11 Wearing celestial garlands and robes, with divine perfumes and ointments, made up of all marvels, resplendent, endless and with face turned in all directions;

12 If the light of a thousand suns were to blaze all at once in
   the sky, it would be like the splendor of that great Being.

13 Pandava beheld the entire universe united, with its manifold divisions, in the body of the God of gods.

14 Then he, the conqueror of wealth, overwhelmed with
   astonishment, his hair standing on end, with his palms
   folded, bowed his head and spoke.

15 Arjuna said:
I see all the gods in Your body, O God, and all kinds of beings gathered there; Lord Brahma seated on the lotus and all the seers and heavenly serpents.

16 I see You everywhere, infinite in form, with many arms, bellies, faces and eyes, but I see no end, nor middle, nor beginning of You, O Lord of All, O Universal Form!

17 I see You on all sides with diadem, mace and discus, blazing as a mass of light shining with immeasurable radiance like the sun, burning like fire, hard to look at and beyond all comprehension.

18 You are the indestructible, the Supreme Being to be realized; You are the ultimate resting place of this world; You are the imperishable protector of the eternal law; You are, I believe, the Primal Spirit.

19 Without beginning, middle or end, with infinite power, with countless arms, with the sun and the moon as Your eyes, I see Your face shining like a blazing fire, burning this universe with Your own radiance.

20 This space between heaven and earth, and in all directions of the sky, is pervaded by You alone, O Exalted One. Beholding your marvelous and terrible form, the three worlds shudder.

21 These hosts of gods enter into You and some, out of fear, praise You with folded hands. The throngs of great seers and perfected ones (*siddhas*), uttering "Hail!", adore You with exhuberant hymns.

22 The Rudras, Adityas, Vasus and Sadhyas, the Vishvade-
    vas, the two Ashwins, the Maruts and the Ushmapas, and
    the throngs of Gandharvas, Yakshas, Asuras and the
    perfected ones, all gaze at You in astonishment.

23 Having seen Your great form, O Krishna, with many
    mouths and eyes, with many arms, thighs and feet, with
    many bellies and with many terrible tusks, the worlds
    tremble and so do I.

24 Seeing You touching the sky and blazing with many
    colors, with mouths wide open and large glowing eyes,
    my heart trembles in fear and I find neither courage nor
    tranquility, O Vishnu!

25 When I see Your mouths with terrible tusks, resembling
    the fires of universal destruction, I lose my sense of
    direction and find no peace. Have mercy, O Lord of gods,
    Refuge of the world!

26–27 All the sons of Dhritarashtra, along with the hosts of
    kings and Bhishma, Drona, and Karna, together with the
    chief warriors on our side, are quickly entering into Your
    fearful mouths with spiky tusks. Some are seen with their
    heads crushed, caught between Your teeth.

28 As the many torrents or rivers rush toward the ocean, so
    do these men of the world enter into Your flaming
    mouths.

29 As moths fly swiftly into a burning fire and perish there,
    so also do these men swiftly enter into Your mouths to
    their own destruction.

30 You lick Your lips, swallowing all the worlds on every side with Your flaming mouths; Your fiery rays fill the whole universe with radiance and scorch it, O Vishnu.

31 Tell me who you are, O Lord of terrible form. Salutations to You and have mercy, O great Godhead. I seek to know You, O Primal One, but I do not comprehend Your ways.

32 The Blessed Lord said:
I am the mighty, world-destroying Time² now engaged here in annihilating the world. Even without your action, all these warriors standing arrayed in opposing armies shall not survive.

33 Therefore, stand up and gain glory. Defeat your enemies and enjoy a prosperous kingdom. They have already been slain by Me, so be merely an instrument, O Arjuna.

34 Slay Drona, Bhishma and Jayadratha, Karna, and the other great warriors who have already been killed by Me. Do not hesitate, fight! You shall conquer your enemies in battle.

35 Sanjaya said:
Having heard these words of Keshava, the trembling Arjuna folded his hands. He bowed again, prostrating himself with great fear, and spoke to Krishna in a choked voice.

36 Arjuna said:
O Hrishikesha, rightly the world rejoices and delights in glorifying You. The terrified demons are fleeing in all directions and the hosts of perfected ones are all bowing down before You.

37 And why should they not bow down to You, O great One, who are greater than even Brahma, the primal creator? O Infinite Lord of gods, O Refuge of the universe, You are the Imperishable, being and non-being and that which is beyond both.

38 You are the primal God, the eternal Person; You are the supreme resting place of the universe; You are the knower and that which is to be known and the Supreme Goal. O Thou of infinite form, by You all this universe is pervaded.

39 You are Vayu (the god of wind), Yama (the god of death), Agni (the god of fire), Varuna (the sea god), Shashanka (the moon), and Prajapati (the lord of creatures), as well as the great grandfather. Praise, praise to You a thousand times, again and again, praise to You.

40 Praise to You in front and back, praise to You on every side, O All! You are infinite in valor and of immeasurable might. You penetrate everything and therefore You are all.

41 For whatsoever I have spoken to You in rashness and negligence or through affection for You as my ordinary friend and companion, being ignorant of Your greatness, calling You, "O Krishna, O Yadava, O friend;"

42 And whatever disrespect I may have shown You in jest, at play or at rest, while seated or while dining, alone or in the presence of others, I ask Your forgiveness, O immeasurable One.

43 You are the father of the world, of the moving and the motionless; You are the object of its worship and its venerable guru. None is equal to You, how then could there be another one greater than You in the three worlds, O God of incomparable might?

44 Therefore, I bow down, prostrating my body, and ask Your forgiveness, O adorable Lord. Be merciful to me, O Lord, as a father to a son, as a friend to a friend, as a lover to his beloved.

45 I have seen that which has never been seen before. I am excited and my mind quivers with fear. Please show me, O God, that other form of Yours. Have mercy, O Lord of gods, O Abode of the universe.

46 I wish to see You again as before with Your crown, mace and discus in hand. Assume Your four-armed form again, O thousand-armed One of universal form.

47 The Blessed Lord said:
By My grace for you, through My own power, O Arjuna, this supreme form has been revealed, full of splendor, universal, infinite, primal, which has never been seen by anyone other than you.

48 Not by the Vedas or by rites or by gifts or by study or by strenuous austerities can I be seen in such a form in the world of men, not by anyone except you, O hero of the Kurus.

49 Have no more fear nor be bewildered in seeing this frightful form of Mine. Be freed from fear and glad of heart. See once more My other form.

50 Sanjaya said:
Having spoken thus to Arjuna, Vasudeva revealed His
own form once more. The great One, having again
assumed His gentle form, consoled the terrified Arjuna.

51 Arjuna said:
Seeing once more Your gentle human form, O Krishna, I
now feel composed in mind and am restored to my normal
self.

52 The Blessed Lord said:
You have seen this rare form of Mine which is indeed
difficult to see. Even the gods are always longing to see
this form.

53 Neither by the Vedas nor by austerities nor through gifts
nor through sacrifice can I be seen in the form in which
you have seen Me.

54 O Arjuna, only by exclusive devotion to Me alone can I
be known in this form, seen and entered into this form, O
scorcher of the foe.

55 He comes to Me, O Pandava, who does My work, who
holds Me as his highest goal, who is devoted to Me and
who is free from attachment and free from hostility
toward any creature.

Chapter Twelve

THE YOGA OF DEVOTION

1 Arjuna said:
Of those devotees who steadfastly worshp you with devotion, and of those who worship the Imperishable and the Unmanifest, which of these have the greater knowledge of yoga?

2 The Blessed Lord said:
Those who fix their minds on Me, who are disciplined in yoga, and who worship Me with supreme faith, them do I consider to have the greatest knowledge of yoga.

3 But those who worship the Imperishable, the Inexplicable, the Unmanifest, the Omnipresent, the Inconceivable, the Unchanging, the Immovable, and the Eternal;

4 Who are even-minded under all circumstances, who have mastered their senses and rejoice in the welfare of all creatures, they too reach Me.

5 The toil of those whose minds are set on the Unmanifest is greater; the goal of the Unmanifest is difficult to attain for embodied beings.

6 But those who resign all actions to Me, intent on Me as the Supreme; who worship Me and meditate on Me with single-minded attention;

7 Those whose thoughts are absorbed in Me, I promptly deliver from the ocean of death and reincarnation, O Partha.

8 Fix your mind on Me alone, let your understanding enter into Me. You shall live in Me hereafter, of this there is no doubt.

9 If you are unable to set your thoughts steadily on Me, then seek to reach Me by the practice of yoga, O winner of wealth.

10 Even if you are incapable of doing this, be devoted to My work. Even by performing actions for My sake, you shall reach perfection.

11 But if you are unable even to do this, then take refuge in My yoga by restraining yourself and renouncing all the fruits of action.

12 Knowledge is of greater value than practice; meditation is of greater value than knowledge; renunciation of the fruit of action is of greater value than meditation; and from renunciation, serenity immediately follows.

13–14 He who has no hatred toward any creature; he who is friendly and compassionate, free from egotism and self-pride, even-minded in pain and pleasure; he who is patient, always content, self-controlled and of firm resolve, with his mind and understanding dedicated to Me; he, My loving devotee, is dear to Me.

15 He by whom the world is not agitated and who is not agitated by the world; he who is liberated from joy, anger, fear and distress, is dear to Me.

16 He who is dependent upon nothing, pure, capable, disinterested, and free from anxiety, he, My loving devotee who has given up all undertakings, is dear to Me.

17 He who neither hates nor rejoices, neither grieves nor desires, who has abandoned both good and evil and is full of devotion, is dear to Me.

18–19 He who remains the same toward an enemy or a friend, in dishonor and honor, in cold and heat, pain and pleasure; who is free from attachment, indifferent to blame or praise, silent and contented with anything whatever; who is homeless, firm in mind and full of devotion; that man is dear to Me.

20 But those who in faith hold Me as the Supreme and follow this immortal *dharma* that has been declared by Me, they are exceedingly dear to Me.

Chapter Thirteen

MATTER AND SPIRIT

Arjuna said: "O Keshava, I would like to know about nature (*Prakriti*) and spirit (*Purusha*), the field and the knower of the field, and knowledge and the object of knowledge."

1 The Blessed Lord said:
 This body is called the field,[1] O son of Kunti, and he who knows these things is called the knower of the field by those who know.

2 Know Me as the knower of the field[2] in all fields, O Bharata. The knowledge of the field and its knower I consider to be true knowledge indeed.

3 What the field is and what its properties are, what its modifications are and whence it comes, who he (the knower of the field) is and what his powers are, now hear all this briefly from Me.

4 This has been chanted distinctly many times by the seers both in various sacred hymns and also in well-reasoned and convincing statements on the aphorisms of Brahman.

5 The great elements,[3] the I-consciousness,[4] understanding[5] and the unmanifest,[6] the ten senses,[7] the mind and the five objects of the senses;[8]

6 Desire, hatred, pleasure, pain, the bodily organism, intelligence, firmness, all this in brief is described as the field with its modifications.

7 Humility, integrity, non-injury, patience, honesty, service to the teacher, purity, constancy and self-control;

8 Detachment from sense-objects, the absence of egotism, and the awareness of the evils of birth, death, old age, sickness and pain;

9 Non-attachment, non-identification of the self with son, wife, home, and such, and constant equanimity toward desirable and undesirable events;

10 Unswerving devotion to Me through singleminded yoga, retreating to secluded places, disliking crowds of men;

11 Constancy in the knowledge of the Self, insight into the object of the knowledge of Truth, all this is declared to be knowledge. Everything that is contrary to this is ignorance.

12 I shall explain to you that which is the object of knowledge. One attains immortality by knowing this. The supreme Brahman, who is without beginning, is said to be neither being nor non-being.

13 With hands and feet everywhere, with eyes, heads and faces everywhere, with ears hearing everything, he dwells in the world, enveloping everything.

14 He appears to have the qualities of all the senses and yet is devoid of them. He is unattached and yet sustains everything. He is free from the *gunas* and yet experiences them.

15 He is without and within all beings. He is both moving and unmoving. Because of His subtlety, He is incomprehensible. He is both far away and nearby.

16 He is indivisible and yet seems to be divided among beings. He is to be known as the sustainer of all beings and also as their creator and destroyer.

17 He is said to be the light of lights beyond darkness. He is knowledge, the object of knowledge, and the goal of knowledge. He is seated in the hearts of all.

18 Thus the field, knowledge and the object of knowledge has been briefly described. My devotee who understands this becomes worthy of My state of being.

19 Know that nature (*Prakriti*) and spirit (*Purusha*) are both beginningless [9] and know also that the modes (*gunas*) and forms are born of nature.

20 Nature (*Prakriti*) is said to be the cause in the generation of the body and the senses. The spirit (*Purusha*) is said to be the cause of the experience of pleasure and pain.

21 For spirit (*Purusha*), residing in nature (*Prakriti*), experiences the modes (*gunas*) born of nature. Attachment to the modes is the cause of its births in good and evil wombs.

22 The Supreme Spirit in the body is called the witness, the approver, the supporter, the experiencer, the great Lord, and also the Highest Self.

23 He who thus knows spirit (*Purusha*) and nature (*Prakriti*) along with the modes (*gunas*) is not born again, regardless of the state in which he now exists.

24 Through introspection, some perceive the Self in the self by the self, some perceive it through the path of knowledge and others through the path of action.

25 Some worship not knowing of these paths but hearing of them from others. They too go beyond death through devotion to what they have heard.

26 Whatever being is born, whether moving or stationary, know that it springs from the union of the field and the knower of the field, O best of the Bharatas.

27 He who sees the supreme Lord dwelling alike in all beings, not perishing when they perish, he alone sees.

28 Seeing the same Lord who dwells in all beings, he does not hurt the Self by the self and he reaches the Supreme Goal.

29 He indeed sees who sees that all actions are performed by nature alone and that the Self is the non-doer.

30 When he realizes that the variety of beings rest in the One and expand from that One, he then attains Brahman.

31 The Supreme Self is imperishable because it is beginning-less and without modes (*gunas*), O son of Kunti. Even though it dwells in the body, it neither acts nor is affected.

32 As the all-pervading ether is not affected because of its subtlety, so the Self residing in the body is not affected.

33 Just as the one sun illumines this entire world, likewise the Lord of the field illumines the whole field, O Bharata.

34 Those who realize the distinction between the field and the knower of the field through the eye of wisdom, and the liberation of beings from nature, they go to the Supreme.

Chapter Fourteen

THE
THREE GUNAS

1 The Blessed Lord said:
I shall instruct you again on that supreme knowledge, the highest of all knowledge, by knowing which all the sages have passed from this world to the supreme perfection.

2 Resorting to this knowledge, they have reached My state of being. They are not born at the time of creation, nor do they tremble at the time of dissolution.

3 Great nature is My womb;¹ in it I plant the seed and from it comes the birth of all beings, O Bharata.

4 Whatever forms are produced in any womb, O son of Kunti, great nature is their womb and I am the seed-giving father.

5 *Sattva* (goodness), *rajas* (passion) and *tamas* (dullness) are the three *gunas* (modes) born of nature and they bind the imperishable embodied soul (*atman*) in the body, O mighty-armed one.

6 Of these, *sattva*, being pure, is luminous and healthy. It binds (the soul), O blameless one, by attachment to joy and attachment to knowledge.

7 Know that *rajas* is characterized by passion arising from craving and attachment. It binds the embodied soul by attachment to action, O son of Kunti.

8 Know that *tamas* is born of ignorance and it deludes all embodied beings, O Bharata. It binds through negligence, laziness and sleep.

9 *Sattva* causes attachment to happiness; *rajas* causes attachment to action; and *tamas* causes attachment to negligence, thereby obscuring knowledge, O Bharata.

10 *Sattva* predominates by overcoming *rajas* and *tamas*, O Bharata. *Rajas* predominates by overcoming *sattva* and *tamas*. Similarly, *tamas* predominates by overcoming *sattva* and *rajas*.

11 When the light of knowledge shines in all the gates of this body, then one knows that *sattva* is dominant.

12 When *rajas* is dominant, there arises greed, activity, enterprise, restlessness and passion, O best of the Bharatas.

13 Indiscrimination, inactivity, negligence and delusion arise when *tamas* predominates, O joy of the Kurus.

14 When the embodied soul dies under the dominance of *sattva*, then he attains to the pure worlds of those who know the highest.

15 He who dies when *rajas* is dominant is born among those who are attached to action. Similarly, if one dies when *tamas* is predominant, he is born again in the wombs of the deluded.

16 They say that the fruit of good action is *sattvic* and pure, while the fruit of *rajasic* action is pain, and the fruit of *tamasic* action is ignorance.

17 From *sattva*, knowledge is born, from *rajas*, greed, and from *tamas* arises negligence, delusion and ignorance.

18 Those who are established in *sattva* go upward, the *rajasic* remain in the middle, and those who abide in *tamas* go downward.

19 When a man of insight perceives that no agent other than the *gunas* is the source of action and also knows that which is beyond the *gunas*, he enters into My being.

20 When the embodied soul rises above these three *gunas*, of which its body is evolved, it is liberated from birth, death, old age and pain and attains immortality.

21 Arjuna said:
By what sign, O Lord, is he recognized who has passed beyond the three *gunas*? What is his conduct and how does he rise above the three *gunas*?

22 The Blessed Lord said:
He does not hate illumination, activity and delusion[2] when they are present, nor does he desire them when they are absent, O Pandava.

23 He who is seated indifferently, unperturbed by the *gunas*, knowing that the *gunas* alone are at work, who remains firm and does not waver;

24 He who regards pain and pleasure alike, who dwells in the Self, who looks upon a clod, a stone, and gold as of equal value, who remains the same in happiness or unhappiness, who is firm and sees no difference between blame and praise;

25 He who remains the same in honor and dishonor, who treats friend and foe alike, and who has renounced all undertakings,[3] such a person is said to have risen above the *gunas*.

26 And he who serves Me with faithful devotion,[4] transcending the three *gunas*, is fit to become Brahman.

27 For I am the abode of Brahman, the Immortal and the Imperishable, and of eternal *dharma* and absolute bliss.

Chapter Fifteen

THE YOGA
OF THE
SUPREME SELF

1 The Blessed Lord said:
They speak of the eternal Ashvattha tree with its roots above and branches below, having the Vedic hymns as its leaves. He who knows it knows the Vedas.

2 Above and below spread its branches, nourished by the *gunas*, with sense objects as its buds. Downward stretch its roots into the world of men, prompting action.

3 In this world, its true form is not perceived, nor its end, its origin or its foundation. With the strong axe of non-attachment, cut down this firmly rooted Ashvattha tree;

4 Then that path must be sought from which, once having gone, one does not return, saying "I seek refuge in that very Primal Spirit from which this ancient cosmic process has flowed forth."

5 Without pride and delusion, having conquered the evils of attachment, immersed in the Supreme Self, with all cravings stilled, liberated from the dualities known as pleasure and pain, the undeluded go to that everlasting state.

6 The sun does not illumine it, nor the moon nor fire. That is My supreme abode and those who reach it never return.

7 In the world of the living, a fraction of My self becomes the eternal, living soul and draws to itself the senses, of which the mind is the sixth, which rest in nature (*Prakriti*).

8 When the Lord takes on a body, as well as when He leaves it, He takes these (the senses and the mind) with Him as He goes, just as the wind carries perfumes along with it.

9 Presiding over hearing, sight, touch, taste and smell, as well as the mind, He experiences the sense objects.

10 Whenever He leaves the body or stays, whenever He experiences sense objects accompanied by the *gunas*, the deluded do not perceive Him; but those who have the eye of wisdom see Him.

11 The seers who strive perceive Him dwelling in themselves; but the ignorant, devoid of wisdom, do not see Him, howsoever they strive.

12 That brilliance which shines in the sun, in the moon, and in fire illumines the entire universe. Know that brilliance to be Mine.

13 Permeating the earth, I support all beings by My energy and I nourish all plants, having become the sapful soma.

14 Becoming the vital fire, entering the bodies of all living beings and uniting with the life breath, I digest four kinds of food.

15 And I have entered into the hearts of all; from Me comes memory, knowledge and reasoning, as well as their loss. It is I who am to be known through all the Vedas. I am the author of the Vedanta and I am indeed the knower of the Vedas.

16 There are two kinds of spirits in the world, the perishable and the imperishable. The perishable encompasses all beings and the imperishable is said to be unchanging.

17 But the highest Spirit is another, called the Supreme Self,[1] who as the everlasting Lord, permeates and sustains the three worlds.

18 Because I transcend the perishable and am even higher than the imperishable, I am celebrated in the world and in the Vedas as the Supreme Person (Purushottama).

19 He who knows Me thus, undeluded, as the Supreme Person, is the knower of all. He worships Me with his whole heart, O Bharata.

20 Thus, O blameless one, this most secret teaching has been declared by Me. By understanding it, one becomes enlightened and will have fulfilled all his duties, O Bharata.

Chapter Sixteen

DIVINE
AND
DEMONIC TRAITS

1 The Blessed Lord said:
Fearlessness, purity of heart, steadfastness in knowledge
and yoga, charity, self-control and sacrifice, the study of
the scriptures, austerity, righteousness;

2 Non-violence, truth, the absence of anger, renunciation,
serenity, the absence of guile, compassion for all beings,
freedom from lust, gentleness, modesty and the absence
of fickleness;

3 Vigor, forgiveness, fortitude, purity, the absence of
hatred, and excessive pride—these are the endowments of
him who is born with the divine nature, O Bharata.

4 Hypocrisy, arrogance, self-conceit, anger, rudeness and
ignorance, these are the endowments of him who is born
with the demonic nature, O Partha.

5 The divine qualities lead to liberation and the demonic to bondage. Grieve not, O Pandava, for you are born to the divine destiny.

6 There are two types of beings created in this world, the divine and the demonic. The divine has been described in detail. Hear now from Me, O Partha, about the demonic.

7 Those who are of the demonic nature do not know when to act and when to refrain from action. They neither understand purity nor right conduct nor truth.

8 They proclaim that the world is without truth, without a moral law, without a God, and that it is brought into being by the copulation of male and female, driven only by lust. How else?

9 Holding this view, these lost souls of little understanding and cruel deeds arise as enemies for the destruction of the world.

10 Clinging to insatiable desires, full of hypocrisy, pride and arrogance, they accept false views through delusion, and act with impure resolve.

11 Adhering to innumerable anxieties which end only with death, considering only the gratification of desires as their highest aim, convinced that this is all;

12 Bound by a hundred traps of hope, giving in to lust and anger, they strive to amass wealth through unjust means for the enjoyment of their desires.

13 "This I have acquired today, that desire I shall obtain, this much I have now and that wealth shall also be mine.

14 "That enemy has been killed by me and I shall kill others too. I am the lord, I am the enjoyer, I am successful, mighty and happy.

15 "I am an aristocrat of high birth, who else is there equal to me? I shall sacrifice, I shall give, I shall rejoice." Thus they talk, deluded by ignorance.

16 Carried away by many imaginings, enmeshed in the net of delusions, clinging to the gratification of lust, they fall into a filthy hell.

17 Self-conceited, stubborn, filled with the pride and the intoxication of wealth, they offer sacrifices only in name, full of hypocrisy and without regard to the law.

18 Clinging to egotism, violence, pride, lust and anger, these malicious people hate Me in their own bodies and in others.

19 These cruel haters, these vile and vicious men, I constantly hurl back into the cycle of births and deaths, into the wombs of demons.

20 Having entered into the wombs of demons, deluded from birth to birth, and not finding Me, they go to the lowest state, O son of Kunti.

21 The gateway to hell which destroys the soul is threefold: lust, anger and greed. Therefore one should renounce these three.

22 The man who is liberated from these three gates of darkness, O son of Kunti, practices what is good for himself and thereby reaches the highest state.

23 He, who casts aside the injunctions of the scriptures[1] and follows his own impulsive desires, reaches neither perfection, nor happiness nor the highest goal.

24 Therefore let the scripture be your authority in deciding what should be done and what should not be done. By knowing what is prescribed by the scriptural injunctions, you should perform your work in this world.

Chapter Seventeen

THREE KINDS
OF
FAITH

1 Arjuna said:
What position are they in who offer sacrifices filled with
faith but ignore the scriptural injunctions, O Krishna? Is it
sattva, rajas or tamas?

2 The Blessed Lord said:
Faith[1] is of three kinds in accordance with the innate
nature of embodied beings. It is *sattvic, rajasic or tamasic*. Now listen.

3 The faith of each person is in accordance with his innate[2]
disposition, O Bharata. A man is made of his faith and,
whatever faith he has, that he becomes.

4 The *sattvic* persons worship the gods, the *rajasic* persons
worship demigods and demons, and the *tamasic* worship
ghosts and ghouls.

5 Those persons who practice severe austerities which are not sanctioned by the scriptures, impelled by hypocrisy and egotism, and filled with desire, rage and violence;

6 Those fools, who torture the aggregate of elements[3] within the body and torture Me also dwelling within the body, know them to be of the demonic nature.

7 Even the food which is preferred by all men is of three kinds, as are the sacrifices, austerities and gifts. Hear now the distinction between them.

8 Foods which increase life, vitality, strength, health, happiness and cheerfulness, which are pleasant tasting, smooth, nourishing and agreeable, are dear to the persons of *sattvic* nature.

9 Foods that are pungent, bitter, sour, salty, very hot, harsh and burning, which cause pain, misery and illness, are preferred by the persons of *rajasic* nature.

10 Foods that are stale, tasteless, putrid, spoiled, leftover and unclean, are preferred by persons of *tamasic* nature.

11 That sacrifice is *sattvic* which is offered according to scriptural laws by those who seek no reward and who firmly believe that it is their duty to offer the sacrifice.

12 But that sacrifice which is performed with the desire of obtaining reward or for self-glorification, know that sacrifice to be *rajasic*.

13 The sacrifice which is not performed in accordance with the scriptural injunctions, in which no food is distributed, no sacred hymns chanted, and no fees paid, which is devoid of faith, is said to be *tamasic*.

14 Reverence for the gods, for the twice-born, for the spiritual teachers and wise men, as well as purity, righteousness, chastity and non-violence, these are said to be the penance of the body.

15 The words that cause no distress, which are truthful, pleasant and beneficial, as well as regular recitation of the Vedas, these are said to be the penance of speech.

16 Serenity of mind, gentleness, silence, self-restraint, purity of mind, these are said to be the penance of the mind.

17 This threefold penance, practiced with perfect faith by disciplined men who seek no personal reward, is regarded as *sattvic*.

18 That penance, which is performed in hypocrisy to gain honor, respect and reverence, is said to be *rajasic*. It is shortlived and impermanent.

19 That penance, which is performed with foolish obstinacy and self-torture, or with the purpose of ruining another, is declared to be *tamasic*.

20 That gift, which is given to one from whom no favor is expected, and which is given to a worthy person at the right place and time, because it is one's duty to give it, such a gift is held to be *sattvic*.

21 But that gift, which is given for the sake of recompense, or given with the anticipation of a benefit in return, or given grudgingly, is thought to be *rajasic*.

22 That gift which is given contemptuously to an unworthy person at the wrong place[4] and time, without proper respect, that is declared to be *tamasic*.

23 *"Om Tat Sat"*—this is recorded as the threefold symbol of Brahman. By this, the Brahmins, the Vedas, and the sacrifices were created in the beginning.

24 Therefore acts of sacrifice, giving gifts and performing penances, as prescribed in the scriptures, are always begun with the utterance of the syllable *"Om"* by the expounders of Brahman.

25 With the utterance of *"Tat"*, the rites of sacrifice, penance and various acts of giving are performed by those who aspire to liberation without expecting any reward.

26 The word *"Sat"* is used to indicate reality and goodness; likewise, the word *"Sat"* is used, O Partha, for any praiseworthy act.

27 *Sat* also signifies steadfastness in sacrifice, penance and gift, and any action relating to this is likewise declared as *Sat*.

28 Whatever oblation is offered, whatever gift is given, whatever penance is practiced or rite observed, if done without faith, O Partha, it is called *"asat."* It is in vain both here and hereafter.

Chapter Eighteen

LIBERATION THROUGH RENUNCIATION

1 Arjuna said:
I wish to know the true nature of renunciation (*sanyasa*) and of relinquishment (*tyaga*) and the difference between them, O Krishna.

2 The Blessed Lord said:
The giving up of actions induced by desire is understood by the seers as renunciation. The abandonment of the fruit of all action the wise call relinquishment.

3 Some learned men say that action should be given up as evil, but others say that acts of sacrifice, gift and penance are not to be abandoned.

4 Hear from Me, O best of the Bharatas, the truth about relinquishment. Relinquishment is declared to be of three kinds, O best of men.

5 Acts of sacrifice, gift and penance are not to be abandoned but should be performed because sacrifice, gift and penance purify the wise.

6 Even these actions should be done without attachment and desire for reward. This, O Partha, is My definite and final judgment.

7 But the renunciation of an obligatory action is improper. Its abandonment due to delusion is declared to be of the nature of *tamas*.

8 Whoever abandons action out of fear of physical hardship, or because it is very painful, performs the *rajasic* type of relinquishment and does not gain the fruit of relinquishment.

9 Whoever performs an obligatory action with the idea that it ought to be done and abandons all attachment and desire for reward, O Arjuna, is considered to perform *sattvic* relinquishment.

10 The wise relinquisher, who is endowed with *sattva* and whose doubts are resolved, does not hate action which is unpleasant and is not attached to action which is pleasant.

11 It is indeed impossible for any embodied being to abandon actions completely but he who has given up the fruit of action is regarded as the true relinquisher.

12 After death, the fruit of action for non-relinquishers is threefold—agreeable, disagreeable and mixed—but there is none whatever for the renouncers.

13 Learn from Me, O mighty-armed one, the five factors in the accomplishment of all actions, as declared in the Sankhya doctrine.

14 The body, the agent, the various senses, the many activities, and divine destiny as the fifth;

15 Whatever action a man performs with his body, speech or mind, whether it is right or wrong, these are its five factors.

16 This being the case, the man of perverse mind looks upon himself as the sole agent and, because of his defect in understanding, does not really see.

17 He who is free from egotism, whose understanding is not defiled, even though he slays these men, he slays not, nor is he subject to bondage.

18 Knowledge, the object of knowledge, and the knower constitute the threefold driving power toward action. The instrument, the object, and the doer are the threefold components of action.

19 Knowledge, action and the doer are declared in the theory of the *gunas* to be of three kinds, according to the distinctions of the *gunas*. Duly hear about these also.

20 That knowledge by which one perceives the one eternal Being in all beings, undivided in the divided, know that knowledge to be *sattvic*.

21 But that knowledge by which one sees in all beings many separate entities differing in their various natures, know that knowledge to be *rajasic*.

22 But the knowledge which clings to one object of action, as if it were the whole, and which is without reason, without true perception and trivial, know that knowledge to be *tamasic*.

23 The action which is done because it is obligatory and which is performed without attachment, lust or hate by one who does not seek reward is said to be *sattvic*.

24 But the action which is performed with great strain to satisfy one's desires or with selfish intent is declared to be *rajasic*.

25 That action which is undertaken through ignorance, regardless of the consequences, loss or injury it may cause to others, and regardless of one's own ability, is said to be *tamasic*.

26 The doer who is free from attachment and vanity, who is endowed with firmness and will, who is undisturbed in success and failure, such a person is said to be of *sattvic* nature.

27 The doer who is passionate, who seeks reward for his actions, who is greedy, who is harmful and impure, who is moved by joy or sorrow, is declared to be of *rajasic* nature.

28 The doer who is fickle, brutish, conceited, deceitful, malicious, lazy, despondent and procrastinating, is said to be of *tamasic* nature.

29 Hear now of the threefold division of understanding and firmness according to the *gunas*, to be set forth completely and separately, O winner of wealth.

30 That understanding which knows action and renunciation, right and wrong action, what is to be feared and what is not to be feared, as well as the knowledge of bondage and liberation, that understanding is of the nature of *sattva*, O Partha.

31 That understanding which mistakenly distinguishes between right and wrong, between what ought to be done and what ought to be left undone, is of the nature of *rajas*, O Partha.

32 That understanding which is enveloped in darkness, which mistakenly considers wrong to be right, and which sees all things in a perverted way, that is of the nature of *tamas* O Partha.

33 But that firmness by which one steadily holds the activities of the mind, the vital breaths and the senses, through unwavering concentration, that is of the nature of *sattva*, O Partha.

34 That firmness by which one clings with attachment to duty, pleasure and wealth, desiring rewards of action, that is of the nature of *rajas*, O Partha.

35 That firmness by which a fool will not give up sleep, fear, grief, depression, and arrogance, that is of the nature of *tamas*, O Partha.

36 Hear from Me now, O best of the Bharatas, the three kinds of happiness, through long practice of which one finds delight and in which he reaches the end of sorrow.

37 That which is in the beginning like poison but like nectar
   in the end, that happiness which is born of a clear
   understanding of the Self, is said to be of the nature of
   sattva.

38 That happiness which springs from the contact of the
   senses with their objects and which is like nectar at first
   but poison in the end, that happiness is known as *rajasic*.

39 That happiness which deludes the self both in the beginning and in the end, which springs from sleep, sloth and
   negligence, is declared to be *tamasic*.

40 Neither on earth nor in heaven nor among the gods is
   there a being who is free from these three modes born of
   nature.

41 The duties assigned to Brahmins, Kshatriyas, Vaishyas
   and Shudras are distributed according to the modes born
   of their innate nature, O scorcher of the foe.

42 Serenity, self-control, penance, purity, patience, upright-
   ness, wisdom, knowledge, and religious faith are the
   duties of a Brahmin, born of his own nature.

43 Heroism, splendor, firmness, resourcefulness, refusal to
   flee from battle, generosity and leadership are the duties
   of a Kshatriya, born of his own nature.

44 Agriculture, cow-herding and trade are the duties of a
   Vaishya, born of his innate nature, while work which
   consists of service is the duty of a Shudra, born of his
   own nature.

45 Man attains true perfection by devoting himself to his own duty. Listen, O Arjuna, how each person finds perfection through devotion to duty.

46 He from whom all beings have their origin, by whom all this universe is pervaded, by worshipping Him, a man finds perfection through the performance of his own action.

47 Better is one's own duty though imperfectly done than the duty of another carried out perfectly. By performing actions in accordance with one's own nature, one does not incur sin.

48 One should not abandon the work suited to his nature, even though it may be deficient, for all undertakings are subject to defects just as fire is subject to smoke.

49 He whose understanding is not attached, who has conquered the self, who is free from desire, through renunciation, he attains the supreme perfection which transcends all action.

50 Learn from Me briefly, O son of Kunti, how one who has attained perfection also attains Brahman, which is the highest state of knowledge.

51 Endowed with a pure understanding, firmly controlling the self, renouncing sound and other sense objects, and discarding passion and hatred;

52 Dwelling in solitude, eating lightly, with speech, body and mind controlled, constantly devoted to the yoga of meditation, and taking refuge in dispassion;

53 Abandoning egotism, violence, arrogance, lust, anger and possessions, unselfish and serene of mind, he is worthy to attain oneness with Brahman.

54 Having become one with Brahman, of serene mind, neither grieving nor desiring, impartial toward all beings, he attains supreme devotion to Me.

55 Through devotion he truly comes to know Me, how great I am and who I am, and having known Me truly, he enters into Me at once.

56 Even though performing all actions, he who takes refuge in Me reaches the everlasting imperishable abode through my grace.

57 In thought resigning all actions to Me, devoted to Me as the Supreme, and taking refuge in the yoga of understanding, fix your thoughts constantly on Me.

58 With your thoughts set on Me, by My grace you shall pass through all difficulties, but if through self-conceit you will not listen to Me, you shall perish.

59 If you resort to self-conceit, and think, "I will not fight," vain is your resolve since your own nature will compel you.

60 Bound by your own *karma* which is born of your own nature, O son of Kunti, that which through delusion you wish not to do, even that you shall do against your will.

61 The Lord resides in the hearts of all beings, O Arjuna, causing all beings to whirl around by His *maya* as though mounted on a machine.

62 Take refuge in Him alone with your whole being, O Bharata. By His grace you shall attain supreme peace and the eternal abode.

63 Thus that knowledge, that secret of all secrets, is declared to you by Me. Fully reflect upon that knowledge and do as you wish.

64 Listen further to My supreme word, the most secret of all. You are exceedingly dear to Me, therefore I shall disclose that which is for your own good.

65 Set your mind on Me, worship Me, sacrifice to Me, bow down before Me, and you shall come to me. I promise you truly for you are dear to Me.

66 Abandon all *dharmas* and take refuge in Me alone. Do not grieve for I shall set you free from all sins.

67 You must never reveal this to anyone who is not austere or who neglects devotion, nor to one who desires not to hear, nor to one who speaks ill of Me.

68 Whosoever teaches this supreme secret to My devotees and shows the highest devotion to Me shall undoubtedly come to Me.

69 There is no one among men who renders more pleasing service to Me than he nor shall anyone on earth be dearer to Me than he.

70 And whoever shall study this sacred dialogue of ours, by him shall I be worshipped through the sacrifice of knowledge. Such is My judgment.

71 And whoever shall hear this, full of faith and free from malice, shall also be released and shall attain the happy worlds of the righteous.

72 Has this been heard by you single-mindedly, O Partha? Has your delusion, born of ignorance, been destroyed, O conqueror of wealth?

73 Arjuna said:
My delusion is gone and through Your grace I have regained my memory, O Krishna. I stand firm, free from doubt, and I shall fulfill Your word.

74 Sanjaya said:
Thus have I heard this wonderful dialogue between Vasudeva and the mighty-souled Partha, which causes my hair to stand on end.

75 By the grace of Vyasa, I heard this supreme secret, this yoga, as it was related in person by Krishna, the Master of yoga himself.

76 O King, every time I recall this marvelous and sacred dialogue between Krishna and Arjuna, I rejoice again and again.

77 Recollecting over and over that marvelous form of Hari, great is my astonishment, O King, and I rejoice again and again.

78 Wherever there is Krishna, the Lord of yoga, and Partha, the archer, there will surely be fortune, victory, happiness and righteousness; this is my conviction.

NOTES

Introduction

1. Mahatma Gandhi, *Young India,* (1925), pp. 1078–1079.
2. "When Time Stood Still," *The Christian Science Monitor*, 10 July, 1965.
3. Helmuth von Glassenapp, ed., *Bhagavadgita: Das Lied der Gottheit*, p. 9.
4. Quoted in: N. A. Nikam, *Philosophy, History and Image of Man.*
5. S. Radhakrishnan, *The Hindu View of Life*, p. 27.
6. Shankara, *Commentary on Brihadaranyaka Upanishad*, 4.4.22.

Chapter 1.

1. Dhritarashtra was the blind king of the Kurus.
2. Kurukshetra is located north of Delhi near Panipat.
3. Dhritarashtra had one hundred sons. King Duryodhana was the eldest son of Dhritarashtra. Here Dhritarashtra is referring to his sons, who are the rivals of the sons of Pandu.
4. The sons of Pandu are Yudhisthira, Bhima, Arjuna, Nakula and Sahadeva.
5. Sanjaya was the minister to the blind king Dhritarashtra.
6. Drona was a master archer who had taught the art to both the sons of Duryodhana and the sons of Pandu.
7. Drupada was the father of Dristadyumna and chief of the Pandava army. He was also the father-in-law of the Pandava brothers.
8. Bhima was the brother of Arjuna.
9. Yuyudhana was a famous charioteer, also known as Satyaki.
10. Virata was the king under whom the Pandava brothers lived in disguise during the years of their exile.

11. Dhristaketu was the king of Cedis.
12. Chekitana was another king and warrior and a friend of the Pandavas.
13. Purujit and Kuntibhoja were brothers.
14. Shaibya was the king of the Shibi clan.
15–16. Yudhamanyu and Uttamauja were powerful warriors in the Pandava army.
17. The son of Subhadra was Abhimanyu, Arjuna's son.
18. Draupadi was the wife of the five Pandava princes and the daughter of Drupada. She bore five sons.
19. Bhishma was an honorable, aged warrior who served as counselor for the Pandava brothers.
20. Karna was Arjuna's half-brother.
21. Kripa was a brother-in-law of Drona.
22. Ashvatthama was a son of Drona.
23. Vikarna was one of King Dhritarashtra's sons.
24. Nakula and Sahadeva were twins, born of Pandu's second wife, Madri.
25. Dhristadyumna, the son of Drupada, was a Pandava warrior.
26. Kunti was Arjuna's mother.

Chapter 2.

1. The term Aryan has no racial connotation here. It refers to the refined qualities of nobility, courage and culture.
2. *Dharma* is interpreted as duty, righteousness, virtue, merit, law, social and moral order.
3. The embodied Self is the individual soul which assumes a physical body. In the transition from infancy through old age, the embodied Self experiences the transition without undergoing any change in itself. Likewise, the soul which passes out of one body and into another remains the same. Change and death come only to the physical body, whereas changelessness is the characteristic of the Self.
4. The Unreal (*Asat*) also means, untruth, non-being and non-existence. The Real (*Sat*) also means truth, goodness, being, and existence. *Sat* is that which is permanent, whereas *Asat* never remains the same.

5. According to Shankara, not even the Supreme Lord (Ishwara) can cause the destruction of the Self because its reality is self-established (*svatasiddha*).

6–7. Here, duty refers to one's caste duty or *svadharma*. Arjuna's *svadharma* is to fight in a righteous war. According to the Hindu scriptures, a Kshatriya who gives up his life in a righteous war goes to heaven.

8. When a person undergoes a moral dilemma and, due to lack of courage, fails to fulfill his duty, he incurs sin. Krishna's words also refer to the moral sense of honor and shame.

9. *Buddhi* has various meanings—wisdom, reason, insight, intelligence, understanding and discrimination.

10. Sankhya is one of the major systems of Indian philosophy, founded by Kapila. Sankhya literally means both number and right knowledge. In the *Gita*, Sankhya is understood as the knowledge of the separation of *Purusha* from *Prakriti*. No theism exists in the Sankhya system but the *Gita* overcomes the dualism of *Purusha* and *Prakriti* by recognizing the Supreme Self as the highest reality.

11. The word *guna* means quality or property. According to the Sankhya system, *Purusha* denotes spirit, soul or consciousness, whereas *Prakriti* denotes nature or matter. *Prakriti* consists of three *gunas*: *Sattva* (goodness), *rajas* (activity) and *tamas* (dullness).

12. Equanimity (*samatva*) also means inner poise. Here, the yoga referred to is *Buddhi Yoga*.

13. The destruction of discrimination (*buddhinasha*) is the failure to distinguish between right and wrong, good and evil. The loss of discrimination paves the way for self-destruction.

Chapter 3.

1. Arjuna's dilemma is succinctly expressed in this question. After all, if knowledge is superior to action, why should Krishna insist that he get involved in this horrible war?

2. Both action and contemplation are necessary for the realization of the Self.

3. Sacrifice (*yagna*) is used here in the sense of meritorious actions which are free from selfishness.

4. Prajapati is the Lord of creatures or the Lord of mankind.

5. Kamadhuk is the mythical cow of plenty, having a woman's head, a bird's wings and a cow's body. Kamadhuk is the fulfiller of desires.

6. After offering sacrifices of food to the gods, the faithful persons will then enjoy the remaining food. Such acts signify rising above self-centered nature.

7. Janaka was the king of Mithila. Janaka was always involved in action even though he had attained knowledge and wisdom. In this way, he set an example for the common people.

8. I have interpreted the word *lokasangraha* as "guiding the people in the right direction." *Lokasangraha* literally means "maintenance of the world." This implies keeping the societal unity which is possible only when leaders provide moral guidance to the people.

9. Karma is inherent in *Prakriti* (nature), which consists of the three *gunas* (*sattva*, *rajas* and *tamas*). The ignorant person attributes acts of nature to the Self. But in actuality the Self is an unparticipating spectator. Egotism results when *Prakriti* is mistaken for the Self.

10. Men should use the faculty of understanding (*buddhi*) to overcome feelings of attachment and aversion, which are impulsive in nature.

Chapter 4.

1. *Maya* means illusion or supernatural power. The embodiment of human beings is driven by *Prakriti* and *karma*. In contrast, the embodiment of the Lord transcends the limitation of *Prakriti* and *karma*. The Lord uses his *maya* to manifest Himself in human form.

2. The four castes are the Brahmin, Kshatriya, Vaishya and Shudra.

3. *Prana* is the life force or vital breath.

4. *Pranayama* is the control of the vital breath. In *pranayama*, breathing through the mouth is avoided.

Chapter 6.

1. The true renouncer is the one who does all action as a sacrifice, not the one who simply meditates and gives up actions.

2. *Brahmasamsparsam* is the ultimate experience of Brahman.

Chapter 7.

1. The eightfold material nature of *Prakriti* is expanded into twenty-four categories in the Sankhya system.

2. The Sankhya doctrine of the independence of *Prakriti* is rejected. The Lord is the ultimate cause of all nature.

Chapter 8.

1. The inherent nature of a thing is its essential property (*svabhava*) and the inherent nature of a person is the individual self (*adhyatma*). The *svabhava* of the Lord is to manifest his spirit in conscious beings. This is called the individual self or *jivatma*.

2. *Purusha* literally means that by which everything is filled. It is the Cosmic Spirit or Universal Self, called *Hiranyagarbha*.

3. State of being implies rebirth.

4. This refers to purging the mind of all thoughts.

5. Hindu mythology narrates that earth's time is divided into four cycles (*yugas*): the Satya *yuga*, with a duration of 1,728,000 years; the Treta *yuga*, with a duration of 1,296,000 years; the Dwapara *yuga*, lasting 864,000 years; and the Kali *yuga*, the current eon, which will last 432,000 years.

Chapter 9.

1. Royal knowledge (*raja vidya*) and royal secret (*raja guhyam*) mean the greatest wisdom and the greatest secret, respectively. The knowledge of Brahman (*Brahamvidya*) is the supreme.

2. Fiends (*rakshasas*) are dominated by *tamas* (inertia) and indulge in cruel deeds. Demons (*asuras*) are dominated by *rajas* (activity) and are characterized by lust, greed and passion.

3. The fourth Veda, the *Atharva Veda*, is not mentioned here. The *Rik*, the *Sama*, and the *Yajus Vedas* treat the subjects of the origin, the sustenance and the end of *Prakriti*.

4. This verse is directly connected with the social doctrine of the Vedas, which women and Shudras were forbidden to study because they were excluded from the Vedic scheme of salvation. But here, Krishna is taking a liberal view by including women, Shudras and Vaishyas in the scheme of salvation, provided they take refuge in Him.

Chapter 10.

1. The seven great sages are: Bhrigu, Marichi, Atri, Pulah, Pulastya, Kratu and Angirasa. The four manus are: Svarochisha, Svayambhu, Raivata and Uttama.

2. The yoga of discrimination (*buddhi yoga*) is also known as the yoga of understanding.

3. Lord (Bhagavan) implies the six divine qualities, namely: omnipotence (*bala*), righteousness (*dharma*), lordship (*aishvarya*), wealth (*sri*), wisdom (*jnana*) and dispassion (*vairagya*).

4. The Adityas are a group of twelve Vedic gods.

5. The Maruts are the wind gods.

6. Of the four Vedas, the *Sama Veda* is mentioned because of its melodious chants.

7. The Rudras are a group of eleven gods, namely: Ajaikapad, Ahirbudhnya, Virabhadra, Girisha, Shankara, Aparajita, Hara, Ankarka, Pinaki, Bhoga and Shambu. These are the most commonly used names for the Rudras.

8. The Yakshas and Rakshas are demigods.

9. Kubera is the lord of wealth.

10. The Vasus are eight in number: land, water, fire, air, ether, moon, sun and the stars.

11. Agni means fire.

12. Brihaspati is the high priest of Indra.

13. Skanda is the commander of the army in heaven.

14. Gandharvas are musicians of the gods.

15. Perfected ones (*siddhas*) are endowed with righteousness, wisdom, detachment and lordship from the time of their birth.

16. Kandarpa is the god of love.

17. Vasuki is king of the serpents.

18. Nagas are the class of snakes.

19. Yama is the lord of death.

20. Garuda is Lord Vishnu's bird.

21. Rama is the hero of the Ramayana.

22. *Dvandva* is compound words.

23. Brihatsaman is a part of the Veda dedicated to Indra.

24. *Gayatri* is the Vedic meter of twenty-four syllables.

25. Margashirsha is the first month of the ancient Hindu calender which partially spans November and December.

26. The Vrishnis are the Yadava clan.
27. Vasudeva is Krishna.
28. Vyasa is the author of the Vedas.

Chapter 11.

1. King refers to Dhritarashtra.
2. World-destroying Time refers here to Ishwara, who is also known as Mahakala.

Chapter 13.

1. The field (*kshetra*) literally means "that which is protected from perishing" but here it refers to matter.
2. The knowledge of the field (*kshetra*) and its knower (*kshetrajna*) refers to the true understanding of *Prakriti* and *Purusha*, i.e., the knowledge of matter and spirit.
3. The great elements are five in number: ether, air, fire, water, and earth. These five elements permeate the whole universe in their subtle state.
4. I-consciousness is *ahamkara*.
5. *Buddhi* is also interpreted as the determining or discriminating faculty.
6. The unmanifest is *avyakta* or *mula prakriti*. *Avyakta* is the cause of *buddhi*.
7. The ten senses consist of the five organs of perception: the ear, nose, eyes, tongue and skin, known as *jnanendriyas* and the five organs of action: the hand, foot, mouth, and organs of excretion and generation, known as *karmendriyas*.
8. The five objects of the senses are taste, form or color, touch, sound and smell. Verse 5 is based upon the twenty-four cosmic principles of the Sankhya philosophy.
9. *Purusha* and *Prakriti* are superior and inferior forms of the Supreme, not independent elements as propounded in the Sankhya philosophy.

Chapter 14.

1. Great nature is Brahman.
2. Illumination is the effect of *sattva*, activity is the effect of *rajas* and delusion is the effect of *tamas*.
3. He renounces all actions and results, except for what is absolutely necessary for the bare maintenance of the body.
4. Faithful devotion is *Bhakti Yoga*.

Chapter 15.

1. The Supreme Self is *paramatma*.

Chapter 16.

1. The Vedic scriptural injunctions are moral ordinances which state what ought to be done and what ought not be done.

Chapter 17.

1. According to Shankara, one's faith does not depend on conforming to scriptural injunctions but on one's character and mode of worship.
2. Innate disposition refers here to individual nature (*svabhava*).
3. The aggregate of elements within the body refers to the bodily organs.
4. Shankara explains that the wrong place is not sacred and is associated with non-Aryans (*mlechhas*) and unholy things.

GLOSSARY

Atman: vital breath; individual self or soul *(atman)* which is eternal, nameless and formless; the divine spark within.

Brahman: the Ultimate Reality underlying everything, the Absolute, Supreme Spirit; one of the manifestations of a personal God in the Hindu trinity.

Dharma: righteousness, justice, duty, law, merit. *Dharma* has originated from the Sanskrit word *"dhr"* which connotes "to bear," "to carry," "that which supports or upholds." *Dharma* is the expression of the Vedic concept of cosmic moral order *(rta)* which operates in individuals and in the cosmos. It is the most important value in Hinduism and is the basis of both individual and social values.

Guna: quality, characteristic, mode, constituent. *Sattva, rajas* and *tamas* are particular gunas in the Sankhya System.

Karma: action, activity, work; the consequences of actions done in the past life; the effect of action. The law of *karma* signifies the operative principle of moral justice in the universe.

Moksha: salvation, liberation, freedom.

GLOSSARY

Om: the sacred syllable, A-U-M; the mystical word representing Ultimate Reality; the divine power and sound.

Prakriti: nature; *purusha* and *prakriti* are the two fundamental principles of nature in the Sankhya System.

Purusha: person, spirit, soul, self which is nonactive, pure, unchanging and eternal.

Rajas: the active principle of existence; mobility; stimulation; sensuous and passionate quality.

Samsara: rebirth, wheel of birth and death, transmigration.

Sattva: Illuminating quality; knowledge; goodness, happiness, calmness, purity.

Tamas: dullness, ignorance, inertia, passivity.

Tyaga: relinquishment, abandonment, renunciation.

Yoga: way, discipline, union. *Bhakti yoga* is the path of devotion, *jnana yoga* is the path of knowledge, and *karma yoga* is the path of action.

BIBLIOGRAPHY

GENERAL

Chapple, Christopher. *Karma and Creativity*. Albany: State University of New York Press, 1986.

deNicholas, Antonio T. *Avatara: The Humanization of Philosophy Through the Bhagavad Gita* New York: Nicholas Hays, 1976.

Murthy B. Srinivasa. *Mahatma Ghandi and Leo Tolstoy Letters*. Long Beach: Long Beach Publications, 1987.

Murthy, B. Srinivasa. *Mother Teresa and India*. Long Beach: Long Beach Publications, 1983.

Nikam N. A. *Philosophy, History and Image of Man*. Bombay: Somaiya Publications, 1973.

Radhakrishnan, S. *The Hiudu View of Life*. London: George Allen and Unwin, latest edition.

Radhakrishnan, S. *Indian Philosophy*. Vol. 1, London: George Allen and Unwin, 1940.

Raju, P.T. *Structural Depths of Indian Thought*. Albany: State University of New York Press, 1985.

THE BHAGAVAD GITA

Deussen Paul. *Bhagavadgita: In vier Philosophische Texte des Mahabratatam*. Leipzig: Brockhaus, 1906.

Edgerton, Franklin. *The Bhagavad Gita*. Cambridge: Harvard Oriental Series, 1944.

Nikhilananda, Swami. *The Bhagavad Gita*. New York: Ramakrishna Vivekananda Center, latest edition.

Prabhavananda, Swami and Isherwood, Christopher. *Bhagavad Gita*. New York: The New American Library, 1951.

THE BHAGAVAD GITA

Roy, Dilip Kumar. *The Bhagavad Gita*. New Delhi: Hind Pocket Books, 1977.

Sampatkumaran, M.R., trans. *Ramanuja's Commentary on the Gita*. Madras: M. Rangacharya Memorial Trust, 1969.

Sargeant, Winthrop. *The Bahagavad Gita*. Revised edition. Ed. by Christopher Chapple. Foreword by Swami Samatananda. Albany: State Univeristy of New York Press, Albany, 1986.

Sastri, Alladi Mahadeva. *The Bhagavad Gita*. Madras: Samata Books, 1981.

Shankara. *Commentary on the Bhagavadgita*. Poona: Oriental Book Depot, 1950.

Stafford, Ann. *The Bhagavad Gita. A New Verse Translation.* New York: Seabury Press, 1970.

Tilak, B.G. *Gitarahasya*, 2 vols. Poona: Tilak Bros., 1936.

Van Buitenen, J.A.B. *The Bhagavadgita in the Mahabharata.* Chicago: University of Chicago Press.